T0336642

For Marga Schreuder-Tromp,
co-founder of the *Centrum voor Conflicthantering*
'Celebrate the differences'

PUBLISHED UNDER THE AUSPICES OF CVC

MODELS FOR MEDIATION

SURVEY AND VISUALS

LENKA HORA ADEMA — LINDA REIJERKERK — JACQUES DE WAART

Preface

The mediator has a splendid profession. Isn't it marvelous to see how parties transition from opponents to negotiating partners, from "I against you" to "Us for a solution"? If things go well they can even acknowledge the other person and leave the conflict, empowered.

However, the mediator's profession is also difficult, in spite of what some people may think. When, at the start of a mediation course, participants watch a demonstration, it all looks relatively simple. But as soon as novice mediators take their first real steps, it turns out to be harder than they thought. Parties do not commit to the process or cannot agree about who pays what. Emotions are building up and communication is usually under par. How to deal with this? Fortunately, the aspiring mediators are given many professional skills and competences to help them supervise the mediation process. And of course, the connection between (conflict) *theory*, *skills* and *process* is essential in mediation. More important even is the mediator's *attitude*. Can the mediator connect with all those involved, and be sincerely interested in what moves them? Skills should not be tricks but honest interventions. Developing this mediator's attitude demands continuous self-reflection, and specific feedback from colleagues, trainers and parties involved. You don't learn that from a book, but only by extensive practice.

The Centrum voor Conflicthantering (Center for Conflict Resolution) gives training workshops for mediation and conflict management and Harvard negotiation courses. Our experience is that mediators profit from a process model that gives something to hold on to, and goes further than showing the main mediation stages. This is why the CvC mediation circle and the MediationWheel have been developed, dynamic models that do justice to the mediation practice. The MediationWheel is the basis for this book.

Linda Reijerkerk as director of the CvC came up with the idea for this book. Together with Lenka Hora Adema and Jacques de Waart, she took up the challenge. Just as in mediation we had an intake phase to determine objectives and lay the foundations. In the exploration phase we explored the various models. Then we negotiated and selected the models, which resulted in this book. We are all three experienced mediators and feel inspired by our profession. This is why we want to share our knowledge by teaching and training people. Of course, we also want to pass on our enthusiasm by sharing our practical experiences. We have written these down for each model.

Why this book with models? Mediation is a relatively young profession, mainly drawing from psychology, sociology, communication sciences and law. In our efforts to raise the level of mediation and to contribute towards the development of our profession, CvC was looking for order in the information coming from these and other disciplines – something to help mediators do their job. A first step was to link the various skills to the structure of the mediation process. By degrees we gained the insight that as mediators we use models from various movements and disciplines – often implicitly. This made us wish to make these choices explicit. *Models for Mediation: Survey and Visuals* is the result.

Why choose to publish in English? Clearly because in different countries our interdisciplinary profession produces different approaches. We would love to stimulate an international exchange of views and practices. This is why we invite our readers to send us mediation models used in their country. These models might be published in the following edition of this book.

We would like to express our gratitude to Caroline de Lint MA, graphic designer, book designer and former Typography Lecturer at the Royal Academy of Art, The Hague, and to Vera van de Seyp, BA, her former student at the same Academy, who together are responsible for the book design. We would also like to say thank you to Heleen van Loon who translated and edited the whole. The great co-operation with these professionals has been essential for this book production.

But most of all we would like to thank our CvC colleague trainers and course participants who are a continuous source of inspiration. Learning is a joy for each of us as it is for the CvC, where we use this joy to educate new mediators and help them towards specializing and gaining more in-depth knowledge. From this love of the profession and each from our special expertise, we have contributed to this book and made it into what it is now. The qualities and insights of each of us enhanced the whole and led to new insights. Almost as in a real mediation.

Linda Reijerkerk
Lenka Hora Adema
Jacques de Waart

Introduction

Paradigms and perspectives, the value of models

ABOUT THIS BOOK   With this book *Models for Mediation : Survey and Visuals* we want to support each of our colleagues in their daily work. Think of a moment that you cannot see your way out and wonder how to continue with your mediation. Or of the moment you notice that the way you are looking at it, is not getting things moving. We imagine you leafing through the book and how the insights you are gaining by examining the various models, give you different points of view, so that you'll see more. You'll see more intervention options so as to get the conflict parties moving. Many models can also help parties to develop those insights themselves. In those cases the model is used in the mediation procedure as a work method[1].

In this introduction we will stress how important self-knowledge is for a mediator. Then, in the second chapter we will introduce the structure of this book which is based on the facilitating mediation process style.

I SEE I SEE WHAT YOU DON'T SEE[2]   As mediators[3] we must depend on what we see. That is where our next intervention begins. What do we expect to get the conflict parties moving? Will we use a pregnant silence, reflection on content, emotions or intentions, or feedback on the way parties communicate? Do we want to invite parties to reflect on their own behavior or do we want them to examine the system they are keeping up jointly? Do we want to speak with conflict parties separately, in caucus, or are we going to give them homework? Or will we perhaps put the question up for discussion whether the right conflict parties are sitting at the table? Whichever intervention we choose, our choice is always based on what we think we are seeing.

MODEL: GLASSES THAT HELP US SEE BETTER WHILE AT THE SAME TIME LIMITING OUR VISION   Our senses are continuously exposed to what is happening around us. This is so much information that we cannot avoid selecting and simplifying. We do that with our own internal models. We have glasses on through which we look at reality. This is why we sooner recognize familiar than unfamiliar patterns. A situation reminding us of an earlier situation quick as lightning triggers a subconscious model so that we can act swiftly. In psychology this is called 'schemas'. Our schemas determine what we see. We do, of course, adapt these schemas continually; we can learn from our experiences and can abstract knowledge from them and about them, in a mental model. What we see as mediators, is therefore also determined by our own mental models. Prein distinguishes four models or schemas: the person schema, self schema, role schema and the event schema[4].

Moreover, we must of course deal with what each participant sees in the mediation, and what their individual mental models are, as they can contribute towards conflict escalation. It is therefore important for mediators to recognize their own models as well as those of the participants.

The *person schema* concerns the model you have of other people in general, the idea you have of mankind. If, in that model, you have the idea that people cannot be trusted, your interpretation of the other party's behavior will be entirely different from what it would be if your person schema were more positive about trusting other people. If the latter, you will interpret someone's behavior more positively and there will be less danger of escalation.

The *self schema* – the idea you have of yourself – also determines how much conflicts may escalate, as the schema contains a norm about what kind of person you are and which behavior is appropriate for that person. This may also determine how much a conflict will escalate. If, for instance, I think it is inappropriate to assert yourself so strongly, then I will sooner condemn a person who does so.

The *role schema* is also a factor in mediation. It involves the behavior we think appropriate between people with specific roles. For instance, how should a father, mother, employer, employee, civil servant or manager behave? Our minds contain models for these roles. Is the behavior inappropriate? Then we will judge and condemn. For instance, 'Mothers should be with their children'. Are they working? Then they must be bad mothers. And where norms clash, conflicts will come into existence. The role schema can therefore add fuel to the fire.

Finally, there is *the event schema* or script that describes the fitting sequences for events in well-known situations. These schemas also determine someone's expectations and norms, and should not be underestimated.

To mediators all these schemas are, of course, well-known and they know how they work. Our mental models influence the way we look at situations and how we deal with them. We interpret from the perspective on which our mental models are based. This is fine as long as what we do, works. For we then have a handle on the situation with which we can quickly structure and interpret the complex and multiple information confronting us. But if people have conflicts and still need to be in a relationship, for instance if there is interdependence, then such models can work as self-fulfilling prophecies. I expect something, based on my role schema; I base my actions on this, and in doing so, invite a reaction that confirms my idea of the role schema. In some conflicts parties can achieve a solution that improves the situation with all schemas involved for each individual remaining the same. This improvement – play the game better – is a *transformation of the first order* (see the Paradigm below). However, there are situations where such a transformation of the first order will not be feasible because underlying convictions are clashing. An actual solution can then only be achieved by looking at these underlying convictions. This involves a *transformation of the second order* – changing the rules of the game – an actual transformation at the level of convictions. Only if we seriously adjust our mental models can we change the rules of the game and then play the game differently. Finally there is the *transformation of the third order*, in which we play a different kind of game. We step outside our frame and find a new game, a new frame. You might say a new paradigm. Or simply, we put on new glasses to look through.

Three paradigms and perspectives on change

Every human being, and therefore every mediator too, bases their actions on mental models. This coherent system of models and theories that constitutes our mental framework and inside which we analyze and interpret reality, we call a paradigm. The word *paradigm* comes from an ancient Greek word meaning 'showing side by side'; hence the original meaning 'example'. This evolved into the meaning 'model' and 'framework'. These are the glasses you use to look at reality, and which determine your view of reality. Take, for example, the paradigms that the earth is round or that the earth goes round the sun. For us, this is a matter of course. But there was a time when these ideas were considered foolish or sacrilegious. The same goes for the concepts of the 'conscious' and the 'unconscious'. Before Freud became known, the idea of the unconscious mind did not exist; now it is taken for granted (see also the various models in the book that refer to it).

Paradigms, according to the philosopher of science Thomas Kuhn, describe the progress of scientific knowledge in a model.[5] If advancing observations do not fit into existing models (or paradigms), the model can be adapted for some time. But sometimes so many adaptations, exceptions to the model, in fact, are needed that a new set of theories – a new paradigm – comes into existence. There will be a new group of scientists adopting the new paradigm but there will also be resistance to and conflict about the change. When the new paradigm, the new way of looking at things, has become dominant, we nowadays call it a paradigm shift.

For the sake of convenience, we divide these larger frames from which we look at reality, into three paradigms. Each paradigm influences how, as mediators, we look at change; for that is what mediation basically is about, getting things moving. The conflict parties are stuck and come to us for movement, for transition. They want to get on. And so they expect something from us – an intervention that gets them going again.

To our opinion it is relevant for a mediator to be able to recognize three ideas of reality or three paradigms: an objective one (there is a reality), a subjective one (the reality is a construct by an individual) and an intersubjective one (the reality is a construct developed in an interaction between the individuals involved). Depending on your idea of reality you will deploy specific interventions to coach parties towards their objective. However, the conflict parties' idea of reality will also influence the choice of intervention (see below for the paragraph about the mediator's paradigm). The *reality paradigm*[6] on the next page demonstrates the connections between the mediator's various ideas of reality, the mediation style and what kind of transition can be expected as intended during the mediation process.

Paradigm (or how the mediator sees reality)	Objective: there is an objective reality	Subjective: reality is a construct by the individual	Intersubjective: reality is a construct coming into existence in interaction
Mediation style	Evaluative	Facilitative	Transformative
Perspectives on mediation interventions	Changing patterns by testing parties' realities using an objective norm	Changing reality as perceived by parties and its interpretation, by reflection and re-formulation	Changing patterns by creating a new perception of reality in the context of the interaction between conflict parties, through mutual recognition and empowerment
Kind of transformation in mediation	First order: play the game better	Second order: change the rules of the game	Third order: play a different game

In the second column from the left one sees the pattern of the first order: 'play the game better'. The perspective is that there is an objective idea of reality. This is the perspective of the evaluative mediator, the deal-maker. According to evaluative mediators, content and process are their responsibility.

The third column from the left shows the pattern of the second order, learning and changing during mediation. The game is the same, but the rules change. The mediator has a multiple perspective of the conflict. The mediator initiates the discussion about the various perspectives, often within the paradigms of the conflict parties. The aim is for the parties to adapt their paradigms and to 'do things differently' because of their new awareness of a multiple reality. The content is the parties' responsibility. According to the facilitating mediator the process is the mediator's responsibility.

The right-hand column shows the pattern of the third order learning and changing, or 'playing a different game', what we also know as transformation. Mediation is here a tool to achieve a new reality. There is no specific thought paradigm. Instead, participants together reflect on their paradigms in order to achieve new points of view for thinking and acting. Both content and process are the responsibilities of the parties. The transformative mediator stimulates empowerment and recognition.

Know thyself

What is the mediator's view of reality and how decisive is it? If mediation is about conflicts and about change, then, for mediators it is decisive what their own personal experiences with their own conflicts are, and how they have learned to deal with these conflicts. We think it is essential for every mediator to know himself or herself. This awareness can be developed in various ways. One way is to get to know analyses and insights from other people. The six perspectives of conflict[7] offer a handle for this and an interesting framework.

You can look at a conflict from the specific conflict dynamics for this specific group of individuals, i.e. how they influence and affect each other (*the systemic perspective*). You can also look at it from the exchange perspective; the mutual interdependence expressed in 'You scratch my back and I'll scratch yours' and 'What's in it for me?' (the social exchange perspective). Then again, the conflict can also be looked at from the inner battle of the individuals involved, e.g. the narcissistic conflicts (*the psychodynamic perspective*). However, the conflict can also be approached as a clash of groups, each with their respective norms and values (*the intercultural perspective*). Another valid approach is to determine which rules in force have been infringed (*the rule perspective*). Finally the conflict can be looked at as the common creation of parties and their intersubjectivity (*the social-constructivist perspective*).

Knowledge of these perspectives makes mediators aware of their own way of looking. It also enables insight into the perspectives that the parties involved use to look at their situation. And this clears the way for the mediator to bring other perspectives to the fore. The models in this book can be considered to broaden the mediator's outlook and serve as a source for mediation interventions. They help you recognize what your model is – whether conscious or unconscious – and how this limits or in fact supports you. Moreover, it helps you get a clearer picture of what you actually do as a mediator and based on what. With this book we hope to help you get to 'know yourself', as the ancient Greeks would have it… which might be your prelude to a paradigm shift.

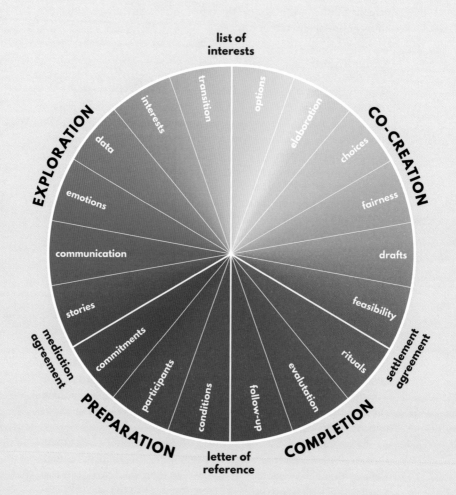

Mediation models and the guiding model, the MediationWheel

Mediation as a model

Mediation can be described in various ways. One way is to use the conditions that must be met, such as confidentiality, parties taking it on voluntarily and autonomously, and the mediator's independence. Another way is to use the essential otherness of mediation when compared to other methods of conflict resolution, which is that parties find (again) their shared values and norms. But, certainly, mediation can also be described as an organic process that can be captured well in a model.

The mediation process model is the guiding principle of this book, which consists of a collection of models that can be used in mediation. Hence all models here are presented according to the structure of the mediation process. Which model can be useful in which mediation phase? And vice versa, which models are available to the mediator in a specific mediation phase? We will say more about the selection criteria later on. First we will now explain the mediation model itself.

The mediation model

The Centrum voor Conflicthantering in the Netherlands (Center for Conflict Resolution, CVC) has always represented the mediation process in a circle, the CVC *Mediationcirkel*[8]. This circle is divided into parts, each illustrating the various aspects per phase in the process. The Harvard negotiation model, also well-known in the field of mediation, not so much focuses on process as on the various principles that promote an effective negotiation. The five principles most used are:[9] 1–separate people from the problem, 2–focus on the interests behind positions, 3–look for options for mutual gain, 4–look for objective criteria and 5–know your BATNA, or, know what your *Best Alternative to a Negotiated Agreement* is.

For the international field there is an alternative version of the CVC circle known as the 'MediationWheel'[10]. This model is the guiding principle of this book. The Harvard principles have a place there as well (see our reference below). You might like to know that the original picture of the Mediation wheel originated in the association with the internationally known peace sign: mediation as a peace-promoting process.

Description of the MediationWheel

In this paragraph we describe the MediationWheel as a model. The division into four parts of the circle of the peace sign indicates the phases of the process, beginning at the bottom and then moving clockwise, *introduction*, *exploration*, negotiation or *co-creation* and *completion*. In fact, the circle model reflects the entire negotiation process.

The differences in size of the phase segments of the circle run parallel with the time required for each phase. This is, of course, only a relative indication of the time needed, whether the mediation takes two hours to complete or two years. Group mediation, for instance, takes longer[11] because the answer to the question: 'Who will sit down with whom at the table?' – the very first section of the process (*Participants*) – may take more than a month. Each transitional stage can be marked with a tangible result of the previous phase. In the model it is a document, both tangible and abstract. Color overrun illustrates the various phases with the three primary colors – red, yellow and blue – and three secondary intermediate colors. Each phase has been divided into sections. These indicate the points of particular interest for the mediator in a more or less logical, but certainly not compulsory order. For example, it is obviously inconceivable that emotions would only play a role in one section of the exploration phase. The mediator will pay attention to emotions at each and every moment. This will happen more specifically during the exploration phase, logically following from the way each person tells their story (*Stories*) and how parties discuss them (*Communication*). (See *Exploration*).

PREPARATION – THE PURPLE FIRST PHASE   This preparation phase consists of three sections. First the *Participants,* where it is examined who will join in the mediation with whom. Who are involved; who should be involved? Which representatives should be there? Should advisers be present, and what about more participants?

The second section is the *Conditions.* Which conditions are needed to be able to start? This is not only about aspects that have been incorporated into model mediation agreements and in regulations such as those of the Mediators Federation in the Netherlands. This is also and precisely about the question which conditions the parties involved need, to be able to opt for mediation. It is the first time that participants and mediators discuss what the former will and can expect from the latter, and what mediators expect from all.

The final section of the *Preparation* ends with the *Commitment,* also sometimes known as the 'psychological contract'. Are participants really prepared to stay the course and will they be able to? It will be a course that will go differently than what has been done so far, and where they will allow the mediator to play his or her role.

MEDIATION AGREEMENT

The tangible result of this *Preparation* phase is the mediation agreement. MFN mediators[12] are even obliged to draw up this written agreement.

EXPLORATION – THE RED-ORANGE SECOND PHASE   Red symbolizes the emotional tension. In the Preparation phase, which seems not to deal with the conflict content but to aim at agreement about the framework (blue), this tension inevitably plays a role too. This is why the color is purple. In the Exploration phase – where the setting has become clear – there is more room for the tension caused by the conflict issues. As the word says, it is the *Exploration* phase, the phase to investigate what the parties' motives are. What is the crucial issue for them? Which to them essential values have evidently been affected? What does the future demand? The six various sections all contribute to the change this second phase is aiming at, from 'parties confronting each other' to 'parties jointly confronted with an issue they must solve'.

Stories offers each party room for their own story and shows up the differences, demonstrating that everyone has their own truth and way of thinking. It also gives an idea of the issues that apparently need attention. Finally it leads to a non-normative ordering of the issues to be addressed.

Communication is about the patterns of communication between parties, and what is needed for effective communication. Obviously the entire mediation process is about communication. Of course, the moment immediately after everybody has been able to tell their story for the first time, is also the moment to pay attention to how parties listen to each other and whether they talk with or to each other (*Harvard 1: Separate people from the problem*).

The *Emotions* section represents the attention that needs to be paid to how parties experience the situation. All those involved have been affected by it, each in their own way, whether only slightly or more seriously – sometimes violently and explicitly, sometimes seemingly without emotions, hoping to keep the situation under control as professionally as possible (*Harvard 1: Separate people from the problem*).

Data is the exploration section where we pay attention to what parties do agree on. These are the facts that they can and want to proceed from. After all, what is a fact for one person can be disputed by another. If it is, it belongs in the *Stories* section and not in the *Data* section. Ultimately *Exploration* is about the *Interests* of parties. Behind every complaint and each position there is a deeper need that needs to be met (*Harvard 2: Focus on the interests behind positions*). While positions produce solutions that exclude each other, interests create a new playing field for more and different solutions.

Transition is the moment that attention is paid to the question if the *Exploration* phase can actually be concluded. Before potential solutions can be really examined it is important that the communal playing field is completely and correctly in the picture. No annoyances from the past, no disturbing emotions should play up when it is time to look for emotions. It must be investigated if there is no more excess baggage, and if there is commitment to look for solutions in the parties' mutual interest (*Harvard 3: Look for options for mutual gain*). In other models this section is sometimes depicted as a separate phase: the tipping phase. Because, however, nothing else happens at that time, we see it as an essential moment in the exploration phase, i.e. winding it up.

LIST OF INTERESTS

The tangible result of the *Exploration* phase is the list of interests which have been taken stock of during the phase. Depending on the kind of mediation, the list may consist of, for instance, flip chart sheets or of a written report of the discussion.

CO-CREATION/NEGOTIATION – THE YELLOW-GREEN THIRD PHASE

To achieve new and different solutions – that is, mutually acceptable ones – the common creativity of parties is vital. The fact that mediators 'only' facilitate, doesn't mean they are lazy, just that they are self-effacing. In this situation nobody knows better what will work, is realistic and feasible than the parties themselves. It is they who know most about their situation and prove resourceful. In this they must, of course, not be hampered by fear; either anxiety about a threat to what is essential and dear to them or fear of the other. Fear being the emotion most counter-productive to creativity, it is essential during the *Exploration* phase to go step-by-step towards understanding, trust and creativity. This is why a careful conclusion of this phase is a point of particular interest. Only then can the *Negotiation/Co-creation* phase lead to viable solutions. The latter phase also has six points of particular concern, illustrated by six separate sections.

Options is the brainstorm moment, to generate as many potential and different kinds of solutions or parts of solutions – as uninhibited and unweighted a brainstorm as possible.

Elaboration is the moment that the various ideas from the brainstorm are developed and specified. The way in which parties proceed in this activity, already gives an insight into which directions the solutions may take.

Choices is the moment where parties, only after the two previous steps, have to choose their options. This sector gives room for the first weighing of pros and cons regarding an acceptable solution.

Fairness is the sector indicating the final moment of choice when it is essential that all parties experience the solution proposed, as fair. This sector not only tests the solutions found against the list of interests; it also pays attention to the question of how to deal with issues parties cannot agree on. If parties cannot come to an agreement about tricky questions, they may probably reach an agreement on the process that can solve that issue or those issues as well. Can objective criteria or fair procedures be found that can contribute towards a solution (*Harvard 4: Look for objective criteria*)?

Drafts is the moment when (part of) the potential solution is provisionally put down in writing. This registration is a tool by itself and makes progress tangible and manifest.

Feasibility is the sector where it is tested if the solution that parties came up with can be achieved. After all, in the flow of the process people come up with many fine and creative solutions but in the end the viability needs to be examined. Moreover, the question is what other people involved (experts and colleagues or relations) might think of the results achieved during mediation. Are they financially, ethically and legally viable? Parties can consult experts at any moment in the process, so such a test quite often will take place earlier – for instance during the *Elaboration* and *Choices* phases. But this is the essential moment for a last check, before the ultimate solution. If the solution proves to be viable and is available for signatures, then this moment of attention for *Feasibility* can also be used to examine with parties the question of how the solution that has been found and that is acceptable in itself, can be improved even more.

SETTLEMENT AGREEMENT

The previous phase results in any case in a joint conclusion concerning the situation at the end of the process. In general there will be a set of points parties agree on regarding the current situation or the solutions in store. A large part of the set can consist of practical arrangements, and partly of agreements about the future process. What the settlement agreement will look like when parties have come to an understanding, varies enormously per situation. Depending on the kind of parties, the issues and the kind of solutions found, the document may be a contract with dozens of pages or just the words of all parties: 'We've cracked it'.

COMPLETION – THE BLUE FOURTH PHASE With the settlement agreement document the process is not yet concluded. The three sectors of the *Completion* phase need to be addressed.

Rituals is the start of this phase. Every process has a beginning and an end that both are the better for a more or less symbolic marking. *Rituals* is about paying attention to the role of rituals in the process, particularly at completion. Depending on the kind of conflict it may be necessary to mark the process of changing with a ritual, to actively let go of the old situation. In business mediations the ritual is mostly shaking hands and maybe a glass of champagne, or special attention for the moment the agreement is signed. In fact, the psychological contract to start the mediation process now is concluded with a new ritual. This is why such a moment of signing the mediation agreement at the start of the process is so valuable.

Evaluation is, of course, essential for completion. A good process benefits from a critical review to see what was considered valuable and what can still be improved. The review can vary from standard questionnaires to a follow-up meeting six months later and offering the opportunity to examine if the solution decided upon has actually turned out to be the solution. *Evaluation* gives both the parties and the mediator the opportunity for feedback from others about the way they performed in the conflict and during the mediation.

Checks, other than evaluative, can also be important, both for parties and for the mediator. At the end of the mediation process, or even later, it may be useful to examine the process. This can be done in a meeting as mentioned in *Evaluation*. This follow-up may also be useful for mediators from the point of view of customer relationship management – always a problem for mediators because of their need for independence and impartiality. How will parties confront future conflicts (with other parties)? How have they experienced mediation in general, and what can mediation contribute in the organization?

LETTER OF REFERENCE

In itself there is no transition from phase four to phase one, mediation for parties being concluded with phase four. Yet at this line between phases in the model, a document has been put in, the *Letter of Reference*. Ideally, clients can give recommendations, and tell others about mediation, now that they have found mediation to be useful and valuable. Why then is the document also placed at the start of phase one? This is because it is important for the mediator to know how parties have arrived at mediation and at this particular choice of mediator. This is useful information about what parties expect and information for how to attune all expectations in the first phase.

Wheel of interventions model

In the previous paragraphs we have used the MediationWheel to demonstrate what the mediation process entails and what the points of particular interest are in the various sectors of the four phases.

cvc has offered thorough intervention training for decades. The various sectors of the Wheel illustrate the various aspects that need to be addressed during the process. These areas of special interest in the end result in an intervention. The rich treasure-house of interventions available to mediators, requires choosing. The many interventions can be placed at very different moments in the mediation process. Yet, each sector of the Wheel has its own particular interventions that are more appropriate for that particular moment. To help select the option or options we are happy to give an overview of the more specific interventions, the Wheel of Interventions.

The previous model of interventions is appropriate for this book with models. At the same time, the visualization approach forces us to limit ourselves to showing this visual overview of all interventions per sector. People who would like to know more about the ins and outs of the interventions mentioned here, what they entail and how they can or must be made, we must refer to the additional literature and training sessions as offered by cvc[13].

We have already mentioned it; each schema or model simplifies reality in order to structure it. This gives the opportunity to broaden one's outlook while at the same time creating the risk of narrowing one's vision. We can therefore safely say, that the more models we offer, the more lines of approach and perspectives are opened, and the wider the view opens, and the more flexible and effective the mediator becomes.

Therefore, with this book we satisfy a wish we have long had, to make the many models that can be important and useful in the practice of mediation not only accessible to the reader but also describe them from the mediation perspective. We include well-known and lesser known models, models that can help with analysis, and models that can be used as a practical work method with clients. We hope that this book contributes to dealing effectively with conflict dynamics[14]. This means the book is not only oriented toward mediators but also towards anybody who would like to enhance this effectiveness professionally.

Choosing models

The choice of the various models has been determined by what we use in our daily work as professional mediators and in our training center. This means that the list of models in this book is certainly not an exhaustive one. To the contrary, there are many more models, and many more potentially useful ones. Please feel invited to send us other models that you have experienced as valuable for mediation.

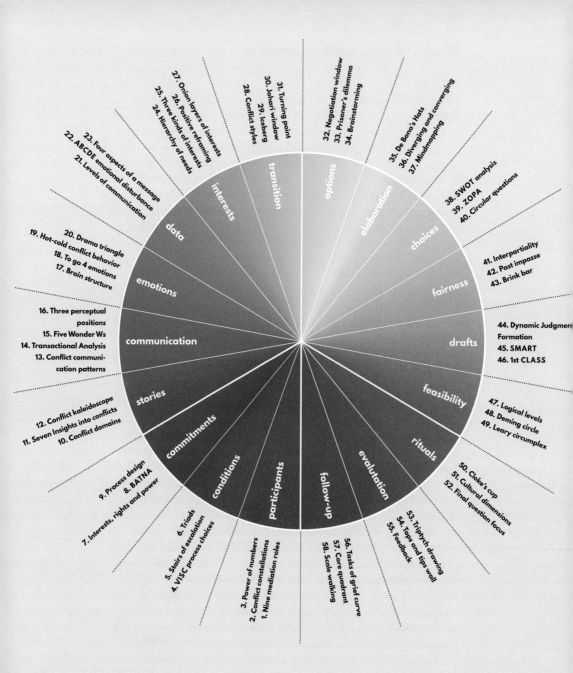

27. Onion layers of interests
26. Positive reframing
25. Three kinds of interests
24. Hierarchy of needs

31. Turning point
30. Johari window
29. Iceberg
28. Conflict styles

32. Negotiation window
33. Prisoner's dilemma
34. Brainstorming

23. Four aspects of a message
22. ABCDE emotional disturbance
21. Levels of communication

35. De Bono's Hats
36. Diverging and converging
37. Mindmapping

20. Drama triangle
19. Hot-cold conflict behavior
18. To go 4 emotions
17. Brain structure

38. SWOT analysis
39. ZOPA
40. Circular questions

16. Three perceptual positions
15. Five Wonder Ws
14. Transactional Analysis
13. Conflict communication patterns

41. Interpartiality
42. Past impasse
43. Brink bar

44. Dynamic Judgment Formation
45. SMART
46. 1st CLASS

12. Conflict kaleidoscope
11. Seven Insights into conflicts
10. Conflict domains

47. Logical levels
48. Deming circle
49. Leary circumplex

9. Process design
8. BATNA
7. Interests, rights and power

50. Cloke's cup
51. Cultural dimensions
52. Final question focus

6. Triads
5. Stairs of escalation
4. VISC process choices

53. Triptych drawing
54. Tops and tips wall
55. Feedback

3. Power of numbers
2. Conflict constellations
1. Nine mediation roles

56. Tasks of grief curve
57. Core quadrant
58. Scale walking

interests
transition
options
elaboration
data
choices
emotions
fairness
communication
drafts
feasibility
stories
commitments
conditions
participants
follow-up
evaluation
rituals

Of course, as professionals we use some models more than others, depending on the case and the people involved in the mediation. These models have either been developed by cvc or the authors involved, or are existing models culled from the fields of psychology, sociology, management, and organization development.

How the models will be presented or expressed

Each model is presented in connection with the part of the wheel where it can be useful. Of course, some models can be used in several parts of the mediation process; if so, we will mention that (see 'Experience'). Each model is presented by three highlights, the three 'E's of excellence. First, you will find the real excellence in the model itself, the picture, or in the way the professional uses it. But for those who want to know more about the model you will find our 3 'E's that tell you more about at which points the model excels:

ESSENCE   Shows what we express as the core quality of the model. It shows what effects are brought about when using the model. The elements the model consists of are checklists, dimensions and, possibly, a summary of some theory behind the model.

EXPERIENCE   Tells you how we use the model, why we have added it to the mediation wheel, or we give you some ideas for using it.

EXPLORE   Of the three 'E's this one is the only verb. So go on and work it out! Find out more about the model if you're interested. We will give sources such as websites to find your way. Please note that for an extensive explanation (the missing E) this is not the book. You will need more. Literature and training will help you to become the model expert and to acquire the final E of excellence.

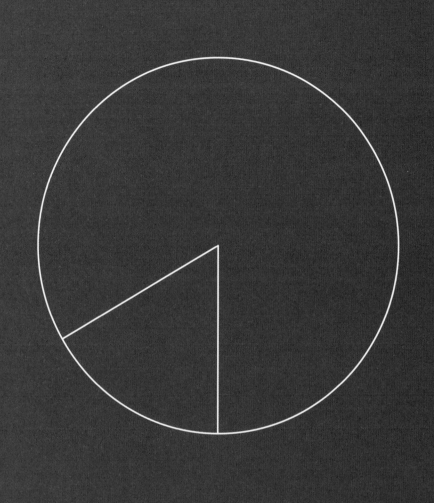

PREPARATION

1   Nine mediation roles

You teach me, I forget. You show me, I remember. You involve me, I understand.   EDWARD O. WILSON

ESSENCE   This model is an analyzing instrument used to clarify the different roles people can play when involved in mediation (in or outside the mediation room). In mediation 9 roles can be distinguished:

- o   PRT   party (A, B, C, D and E).
- o   REP   representative (F and G)
- o   COA   coach (H and I)
- o   EXP   expert advisor (J, K and L).
- o   CON   third contractor (M)
- o   REF   referrer (N)
- o   ABS   absent stakeholder (O and P)
- o   INV   passively involved (Q)
- o   MED   mediator (R).

This instrument helps to analyze the conflict system for a better understanding of the various influences during mediation. This model also helps mediators to prepare the first session, by giving them a perspective on who will or needs to be at the mediation table and in what role. It is therefore very useful for group mediation and multi-party mediations. First, it gives insight into the various responsibilities and manages the expectations. Second, it gives all those involved a clear picture of everyone's role. Third, it helps to find out who is needed at the mediation table when, with whom, about what and in what role.

EXPERIENCE   We use the model especially in multi-stakeholder situations. It is especially helpful in an intake caucus as well as during the rest of the mediation process. For instance it might be that an advisor needs to be asked to join or a third party has to be taken into account in the negotiation phase. The definition of these different roles can be used as a checklist for finding out in what way someone is connected to the conflict situation and in what way that role can change during the process.

EXPLORE   Thiebout, M., K. van Oyen, L.J. Reijerkerk and J.A.Th.M. de Waart. *Groepsmediation: Dynamiek, procesontwerp en werkvormen.* The Hague: SDU Publishers, 2nd edition, 2015.

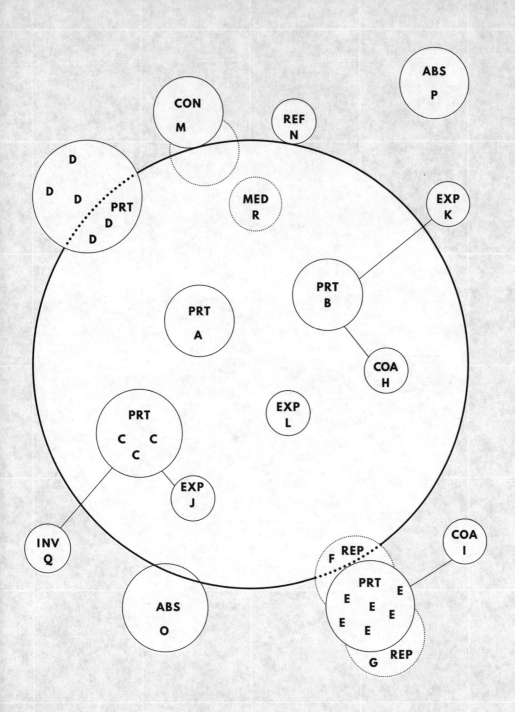

2   Conflict constellations

Social cohesion was built into language long before Facebook and LinkedIn and Twitter – we're tribal by nature. PETER GUBER

ESSENCE   Conflict constellations refer to the way participants relate to each other in terms of number and cohesion. This model helps us understand the dynamics between participants in a multi-party mediation. The number of people present at the mediation table clearly has an influence on the conflict dynamics. A boardroom of 6 directors having a dispute has a different interaction than two teams of a ministry department who are in conflict. The number of people and the cohesion within these groups is often expressed and reinforced by group think: 'we' against 'them'. The cohesion has, of course, an impact on the mediation dynamics: some members may feel forced not to disclose certain information or not to agree with certain outcomes. The model shows 7 constellations, ranging from a 2-parties-2-persons setting to a multiparty setting of 2 or more teams in conflict. Even *within* a party a sub-party may be present, as may be the case in a dispute between the CEO and the labor council/union, with the chair of the Union also having an internal conflict with his co-chair.

EXPERIENCE   We use this model as an analytical tool, in multi-party mediations. It helps us to get some insight into the group dynamics. The model presents the situation at a specific moment, for instance at the start of a mediation. However, it is also a dynamic model. Cohesion between or within parties may change and – consequently – the constellation may gradually change into another one. In our preparation for a next session we use this model as an analyzing tool to see if something has changed. For instance, there was a multiparty conflict about the location of a wind farm between representatives of local, provincial and national authorities, and a group of 20 households who were against the farm (no 4 constellation). However, during the mediation one family within this group of households changed their minds; so a combination of numbers 4 and 5 constellations developed. Needless to say, the mediator may have to redirect his process design (see also model 9, *Process design*) and act accordingly.

EXPLORE   Thiebout, M., K. van Oyen, L.J. Reijerkerk and J.A.Th.M. de Waart. *Groepsmediation: Dynamiek, procesontwerp en werkvormen.* The Hague: SDU Publishers, 2nd ed., 2015.

1 two individuals opposed to each other

2 several individuals opposed to each other

3 individual opposed to a group

4 groups opposed to each other

5 individual within a group

6 several individuals within a group

7 several groups within a group

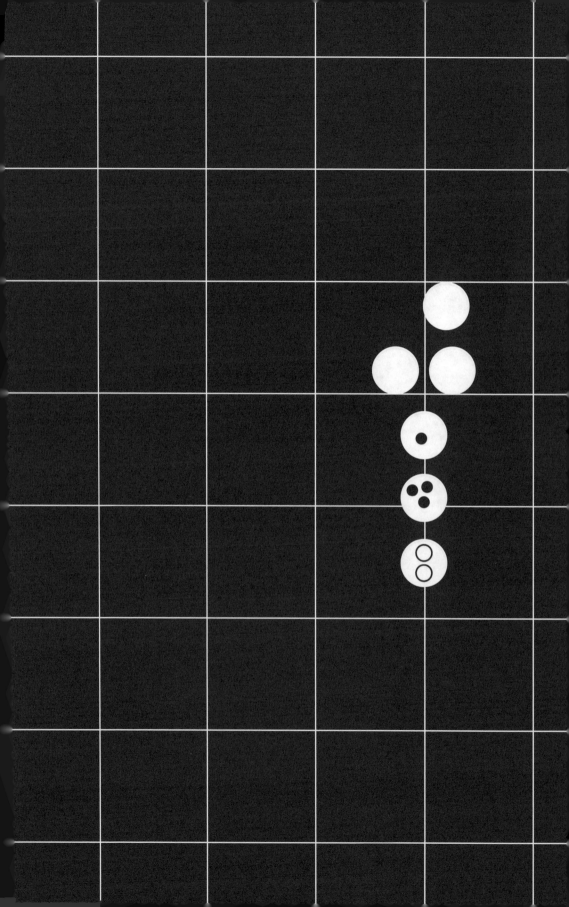

3   Power of numbers

ESSENCE   The model highlights the position of stakeholders in a conflict. What is the relationship between the representative and the dependence group? Is the group sending the representative on stage to pronounce their statements, arguments and wishes? Or is the representative merely the senator who has to convince his followers? In other words, is he the Commander-in-Chief or an actual representative? Linked to this is his level of authority. The mediator, of course, has to investigate what the parties' level of authority is, to be able to decide what steps to take in this mediation. Apart from positions, the *number* of people of which a party consists is also important; this counts both for the number of people present at the mediation table, and for the followers or the constituency that a party is representing. This model investigates the position of stakeholders and a potential power imbalance in number, status, and – thus – influence. The outcome of this analysis could influence the playing field in the mediation. The mediator can use this model at any time in the mediation process, but preferably in the intake phase, using a set of questions that gives insight into each stakeholder's strengths and weaknesses:

o   Is it an open group or have boundaries been set?
o   What is the internal communication like?
o   What is the management style?
o   What is the decision-making structure?

This model can be linked to Euwema's *7 Insights* (model 11) and to the *Conflict constellations* model (model 2).

EXPERIENCE   Clearly, this tool is interesting for group mediations or multi-party mediations. But also for two-party mediations it is interesting to investigate who else – apart from those at the mediation table – is involved in the dispute. Often the employees' spouses are more conflict parties than the employees themselves. We recall numerous mediations where the spouse (not formally, but in practice the actual disputant) was not present at the mediation, but anxiously waiting at home to see what news his husband or wife was coming home with. The 'poor' disputant then had to deal with another conflict at home if the result was not deemed good enough.

EXPLORE   Glasl. F. *Konfliktmanagement: Ein Handbuch für Führungskräfte, Beraterinnen und Berater.* Wien: Trigon, 2004.
Thiebout M., K. van Oyen, L. J. Reijerkerk and J.A.Th.M. de Waart. *Groepsmediation, Dynamiek, procesontwerp en werkvormen.* SDU Publishers, 2nd ed., 2015.

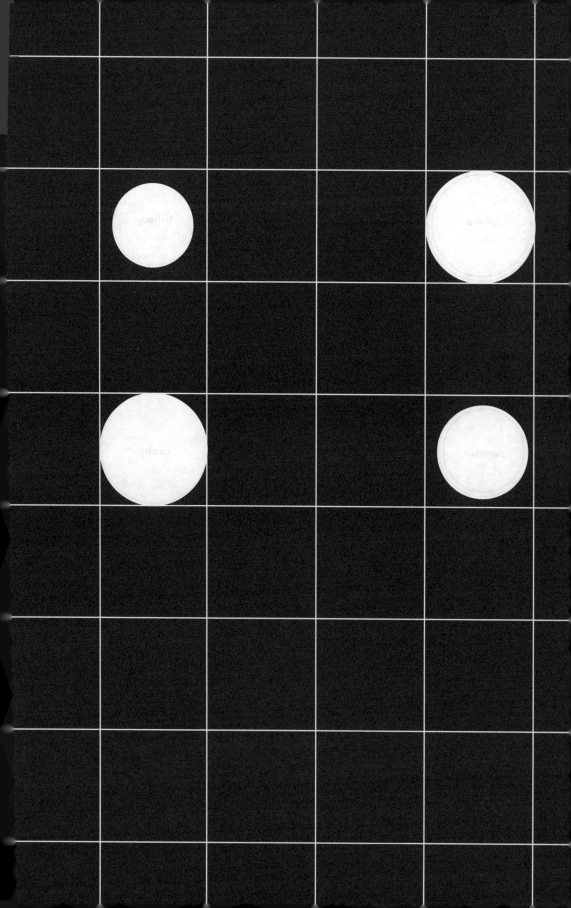

4   VISC process choices

ESSENCE   This model, developed by Paul Gibson and Frank Handy, helps mediators to make process choices. It illustrates the challenge offered by having to maintain the balance between the four fundamental principles of mediation which are related to the tensions of remaining neutral, i.e. Voluntariness, Independence, Self-determination and Confidentiality (VISC). These tensions arise because neutrality and objectivity are affected by:

o   our own feelings and emotions *(personality and disposition)*
o   opinions, beliefs, values, prejudices and preferences *(norms)*
o   thought and assumptions *(cognition and judgments)*
o   life experience and past history *(biases are triggered)*
o   views of human rights and social justice
o   social competence *(empathy and communications)*
o   patterns of thinking in the process *('lost in the fog')*
o   conscious and unconscious biases.

EXPERIENCE   As a mediator you sometimes may feel that your neutrality is at stake. But what exactly is neutrality? The VISC model helps with self-reflection. Is the voluntariness of parties being threatened? Do participants feel free to leave the mediation table or do they feel under pressure somehow through my interventions? And what about ourselves? What about our impartiality and independence? Do we have biases, do we dislike one of the parties and is that reflected in our behavior? How is self-determination of parties guaranteed: is party autonomy being safeguarded? Do mediator and/or the parties indeed observe confidentiality? And if the parties do not observe confidentiality, are we initiating a dialogue with them on this issue?

Case: in a multi-party mediation about a waste disposal site we had the feeling that our neutrality was somehow undermined, but the reason was not clear to us. We had followed the *Rules of Conduct*, so what was happening? We used the VISC model to investigate the different aspects more systematically and realized the following. One of the parties, James, wanted to withdraw and we were trying everything we could to change this. In other words, we were threatening James' self-determination. As soon as we realized this we could change our attitude and behavior. We feel, however, that the model lacks one aspect: transparency. If the mediator is not transparent in everything he does, his neutrality might be at stake.

EXPLORE   Gibson, P.R., 'Ch. 5: Mediator Bias'. In: *How to Master Commercial Mediation?*, Richbell, D., Bloomsbury, UK, 2014.

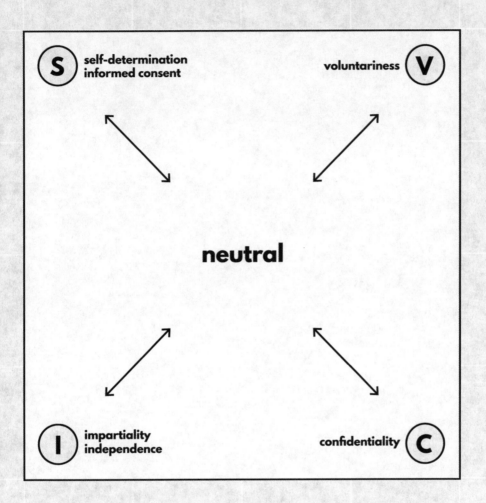

5   Stairs of escalation

Between uncontrolled escalation and passivity, there is a demanding road of responsibility that we must follow.

DOMINIQUE DE VILLEPIN

ESSENCE   Conflict escalation is not a sudden event, but develops in stages: from win-win to win-lose to lose-lose. The model thus comprises 3 main stages: **win-win/win-lose/lose-lose**. Every stage is divided into three sub-stages where particular conflict behavior is described, making nine sub-stages in all. It is important to know that there is always a 'threshold', a particular (conflict) event, which has made people fall into the next stage, in particular into the main stages *win-win*, *win-lose* or *lose-lose*. Quite often participants still know exactly what the event was: 'Mediator, when he had written that letter, I lost my rag!' This is why it is important for the mediator to examine these key situations together with the persons involved. Apart from this the model is particularly suitable for examining the scale of the escalation; mediation with parties that are in the *lose-lose* stage is particularly difficult. The main sphere of activity for the mediator is somewhere between the main stages of *win-win* and *win-lose*. The model can be used as an analytic tool in the intake or *exploration phase* to assess the parties' commitment and to see what the chances are for successful mediation, by identifying the level of conflict escalation.

EXPERIENCE   This is our favorite model in the *exploration phase*, though it has its value for the intake phase as well. In case of a high escalation conflict we may even show parties the (simplified) model and ask them which stage they think they are at and whether that is what they want. This helps them understand a great deal. You may often see that one party has fallen further down the Escalation stairs than the other; this will give rise to some interesting questions the mediator can ask, such as questions about the way the conflict developed, and the parties' interaction. Courts or government services referring parties to mediation will use the model to determine the level of escalation implicitly or explicitly (see also model 11, *Seven Insights into conflicts*). This is what they base their conclusions on as to whether there is some point in a referral to the mediator.

EXPLORE   Glasl, F. (1982) *'The process of conflict escalation and roles of third parties'* in G.B.J. Bomers and R.B. Peterson, (eds) Conflict management and indistriual relations, (pp. 119-140). The Hague: Kluwer Nijhoff Publishing.

1
Positions hardening

Discussion hardening

Impasse

Mutual understanding no longer self-evident

Shielding yourself

Cooperative conflict solving

Awareness of tension

Selective attention

No paralysis yet

2
Debates

Intellectual force

Competition

Feeling of superiority

Polarization

Style of the debate

Scoring

Provoking irritation

Poking fun

Black & white thinking

3
Actions

Actions, not words

Non-verbal communication

Matter of prestige

No retraction

Less empathy

No shared responsibility

No faith in solutions

4
Images Stereotypes, caricatures

Self-fulfilling prophecy

Conflict escalation

Need for sympathy

Winning people over to your side

Coalitions

Black or white image

Double bind by contradictory assignments

5
Loss of face

Attack on public image and loss of faith

Foul play

Exposure

Giving the cold shoulder

Moral outrage

Ostracizing

Principles, ideologies

6
Strategies of threat

Stringent requirements

Panic impulses

Sanctions

Stress

Ultimatums

7
Retaliatory acts

Counterpart becomes object/ enemy

Violence

Harm counterpart, prepared to suffer damage yourself

8
Destruction

Systematic destructive campaigns

Paralyze enemy

Fragmentation of counterpart

9
Into the abyss together

Into the abyss together

Point of no return

Phase 1: win-win

Parties are aware of tensions but control them. Co-operation is the objective, but there are non-professional annoyances

Phase 2: win-lose

Non-professional annoyances have the upper hand; social-emotional conflict; winning or losing is the main issue

Phase 3: lose-lose

No more avoidance of fierce confrontations; counterparts do not treat each other as people anymore

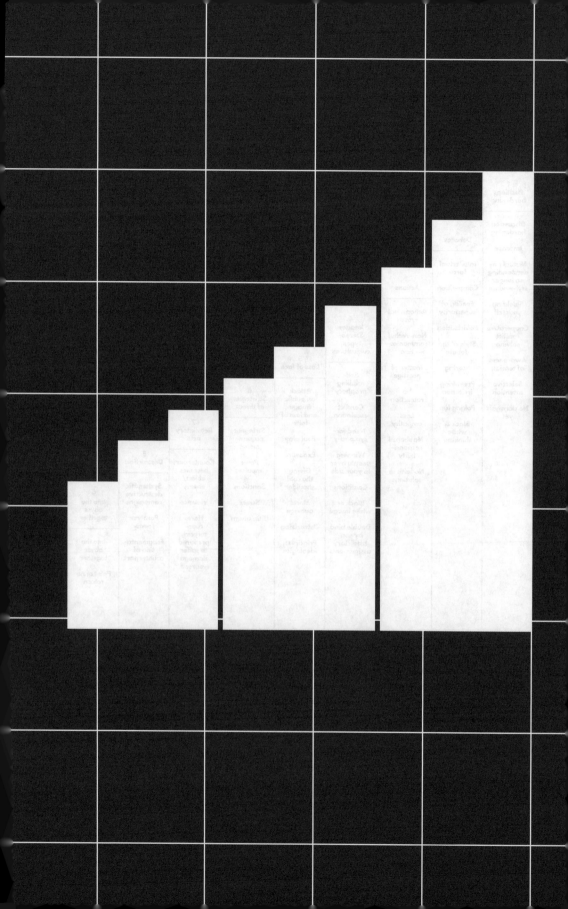

6 Triads

ESSENCE The triad is a tool for analyzing the conflict system. The triangle with its symbols for relationships with a positive charge ('friend', double line) and with a negative charge ('enemy', opposing arrows) offers an instrument for visualizing inter-human relations in organizations or families. The system consists of combined and linked triangles, demonstrating how in interactions positive ('friend') and negative ('enemy') attitudes and types of behavior affect other relationships, influenced by feelings of loyalty. It also helps with hypotheses about the charge of relationships not yet or not sufficiently clear. If, for instance, it is evident that the CEO has a good relationship with his immediate assistant, and that the CEO is also in conflict with his three members of the board of directors, the triad helps hypothesize that the relationship between the CEO assistant and the directors may also be an issue. Moreover, working with triads enables the parties concerned to gain insight into their context of positively and negatively charged relationships. We can discern two types of triads, balanced and unbalanced. Balanced triads: **The friend of my friend is my friend / The enemy (B) of my friend (C) is my enemy (I) / The enemy (B) of my enemy (C) is my friend (II) / The friend of my enemy is my enemy.** Unbalanced triads – e.g. **the friend (B) of my enemy is my friend (III)** – will put a person under pressure to create balance again. This influences relationships. The model thus illustrates positive and negative personal relations and helps to find everyone's position in the conflict situation. If change is needed, the drawing of the figure of the system helps create awareness of a mutual responsibility (see model 40, *Circular questions*).

EXPERIENCE Questions suitable to this approach are directed towards gaining insight into how subjects describe their relationships in this context. These so-called 'circular questions' are not aimed at clarifying the content of the conflict but rather at how everybody sees the roles of the other subjects in this particular conflict situation. In a joined session, drawing the figure together with the participants is a powerful instrument to discover in what way everyone is related to the others. It should be stressed that individual interviews beforehand are important tools both to accustom parties to the type of questions and to create commitment and support for this specific approach.

EXPLORE Catwright, D. and F. Harary. *'Structural balance: a generalization of Heider's theory'.* Psychological Review 63 (1956): 277-293.

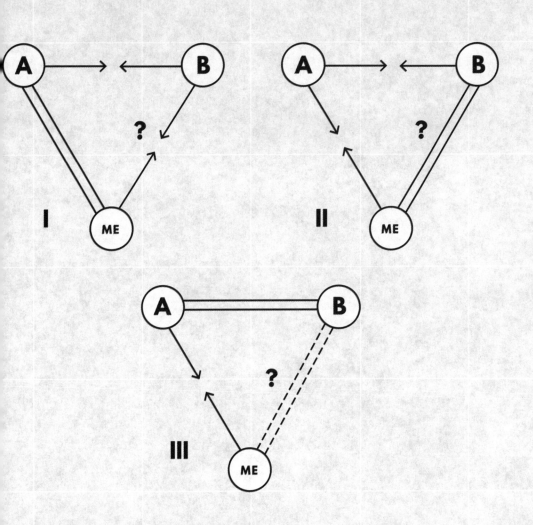

I

II

III

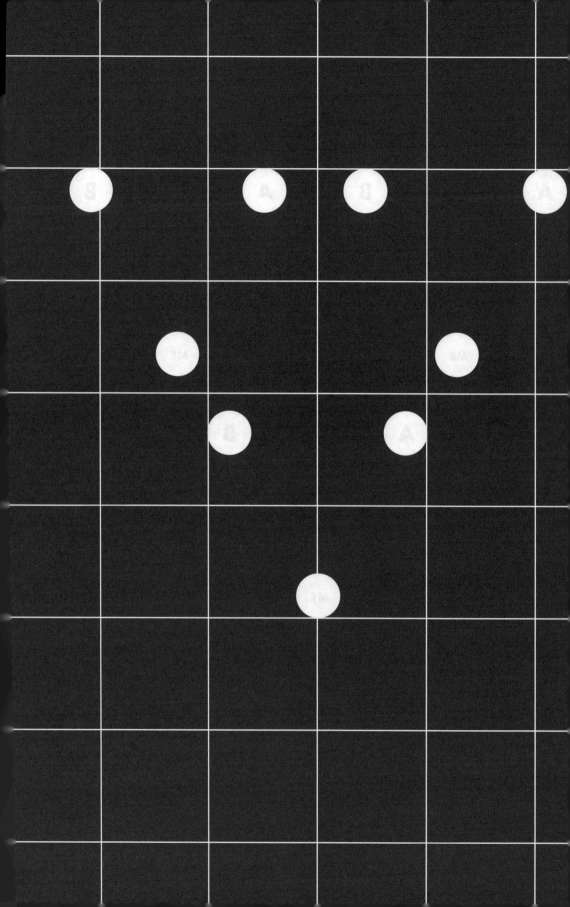

7 Interests, rights and power

ESSENCE This model of interests, rights and power shows the perspectives of conflict parties and what is needed to move from a distressed to an effective dispute resolution system. It describes the strategic negotiation options as well. This concept makes participants aware of their conflict behavior and their best alternative to a negotiated agreement (model 8, BATNA). It helps parties to make a deliberate choice for mediation. By creating understanding you can make them choose a specific strategy more consciously, particularly by showing the roles of power and justice for the various positions of parties, in their specific situation. If as a mediator you switch the focus to underlying interests, parties gain more insight into how the results can vary, using power, legal actions, or a focus on interests. *Rights* can be seen as standards of legitimacy and fairness – such as equality and precedent – defined through law or contract. *Power* is the ability to make people do something they otherwise would not do, by, for instance, threatening with imposing costs, withholding certain benefits or acts of aggression. *Interests* are the needs, desires, concerns and fears underlying the position of a conflict party. The basic (instinctive) reaction in a conflict primarily focuses on fight or flight, using *power* when resistance is expected. If it becomes clear that the use of power will not lead to the result desired, the next step is checking which legal actions can be useful (the rights perspective). In some way using a legal procedure is a matter of power as well. The conflict party is not focusing on interests, then. When, however, the mediator starts to explore the interests, legal and power alternatives are recognized.

EXPERIENCE Mediators take all three elements – rights, power and interests – into account. When preparing, we anticipate what power and rights may imply for the strategic choices parties have made. We look for the interests and concerns behind the strategic choices, trying to integrate them into the negotiation. Exploring with parties what legal or power solutions can and cannot bring, we check whether these will be acceptable alternatives to a negotiated agreement. Quite often they are not. Therefore we recommend you not only to focus on interests. Be aware of power and rights perspectives as important elements in a conflict.

EXPLORE Ury, W.L., Jeanne M. Brett and Stephen B. Goldberg. 'Three Approaches to Resolving Disputes: Interests, Rights, and Power in *Negotiation Fundamentals*'. In: *Getting Disputes Resolved* by William L. Ury et al., 3-19. San Francisco: Jossey-Bass Inc, 1988.

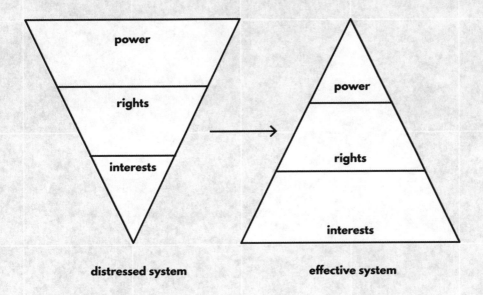

distressed system　　　　**effective system**

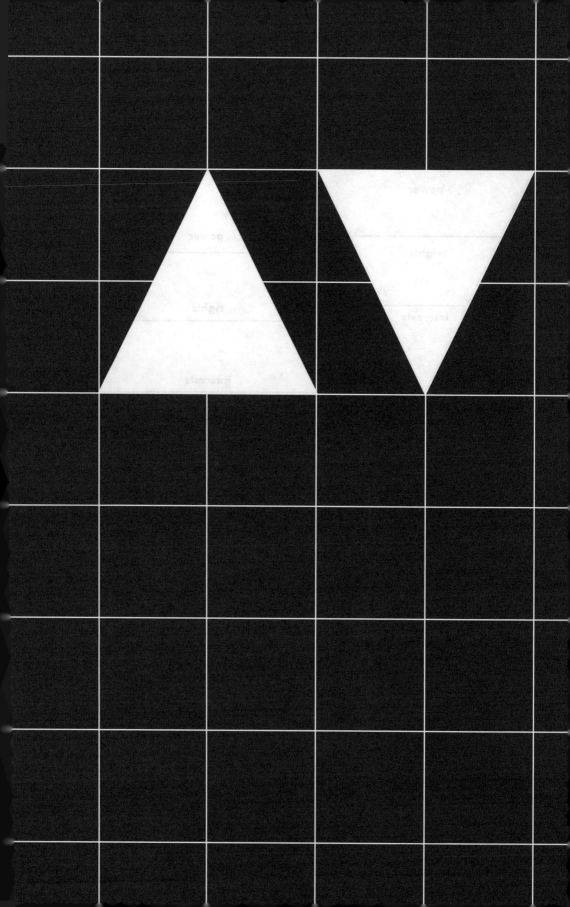

8 BATNA

ESSENCE   Your Best Alternative To a Negotiated Agreement: that is your BATNA. You would like to get something better than what you would have without negotiations and without the mediation process. You could also say that BATNA is your safety net where you land if the negotiations fail and you miss out on what you had already achieved or thought to have gained. But BATNA is specifically used to get to know which negotiation result you should accept; you should gain from the negotiation or you would not be doing it or agreeing to its result. The norm with which a party in a conflict operates and looks at a proposal, is their BATNA. The BATNA model is continuously in play during a mediation process, but it is particularly relevant during

o   the start of the mediation
o   the transition period
o   and before completing the process.

EXPERIENCE   First, as a mediator you should stimulate the parties to clarify their BATNA for themselves. You can do this in caucus. In fact, conflict coaching is added here to the mediation caucus tool box. For instance, we ask each of the conflict parties separately and in caucus to list the results they think they can achieve or have already achieved if the negotiations fail. The BATNA interview can also prepare for the brainstorm stage, and it can refresh what was presented during the brainstorm. Moreover, new aspects may emerge in caucus: the hidden agenda or in any case those options the party concerned was not willing to share. Second, you could usefully ask the parties to brainstorm the possibilities to improve these first ideas and to convert them into practical solutions. Finally, it can sometimes be helpful in caucus to have the parties prepare and think about their best options and outcomes. After these three stages BATNA becomes very tangible and useful as a reference point during negotiations. Our experience is that parties gain confidence in the negotiation process if they have first done this work in caucus. This confidence speeds up the negotiation process. After all, an insecure party is a bad negotiator, which then leads to an unsatisfactory result or no result at all (see model 39, ZOPA).

EXPLORE   Fisher, Roger, William L. Ury and Bruce Patton. *Getting to Yes: Negotiating Agreement Without Giving In.* New York: Penguin Books, 2011.

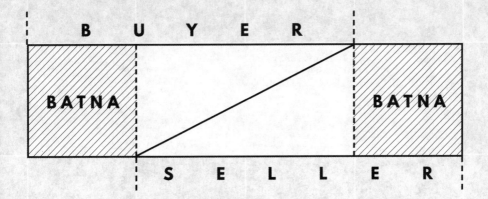

9 Process design

ESSENCE The model is a tool for analyzing a conflict situation systematically, and a guideline for designing the mediation process before and during mediation. Being well prepared by choosing the most effective approach for the specific dynamics of a specific situation gets you off to a good start. The effect of this designing at first seems to be a paradox; the more you design your approach, the more you become flexible in it and feel free to do what is needed instead of what has been prepared. Considered reflection beforehand creates room for new possibilities. Systematically thinking things through also offers a frame of reference during the hectic process. The design has the following components:

o   mediation structure (the entire mediation process from start to finish)
o   work processes – within the mediation structure – with a process activity of specific duration, such as the intake interview or the caucus (This process starts and ends at appointed times and there is agreement about the preconditions for that activity.)
o   forms of activity (Within the framework of mediation phases and the work processes chosen, the mediator uses various forms of activity – specific ways to go to work within one work process, such as using a planning board, homework exercise or dividing into subgroups.)
o   interventions (A concrete action by the mediator here and now to influence the group dynamics. It is a specific question or intervention with that specific work method in that specific situation.)
o   mediation participants (who takes part in the mediation, when and in what role?) (see model 1, *Nine mediation roles*).

EXPERIENCE Preparing the approach by thinking of all the different steps to take, helps to become aware of unconscious or implicit choices and makes you more creative, using new work methods. However, working with process design needs preparation. Especially in complex group mediations it is a useful tool for a constructive approach to group dynamics. Various forms of activity are available, each with their pros and cons. Therefore, knowledge of these activities and experience with them make mediators more flexible in dealing with group dynamics. For instance, activities bringing about the equal contribution of group members prevent that dominant players monopolize the discussion. On the other hand, there are activities that promote the appearance of one group representative.

EXPLORE Thiebout, M., K. van Oyen, L.J. Reijerkerk and J.A.Th.M. de Waart. *Groepsmediation: Dynamiek, procesontwerp en werkvormen.* The Hague: SDU Publishers, 2nd edition, 2015.

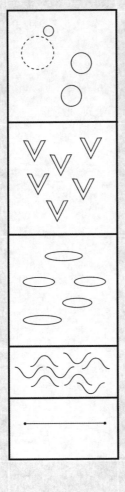

○ mediator
○ mediation participants
V intervention
⬭ form of activity
⌣ work process
•—• mediation structure

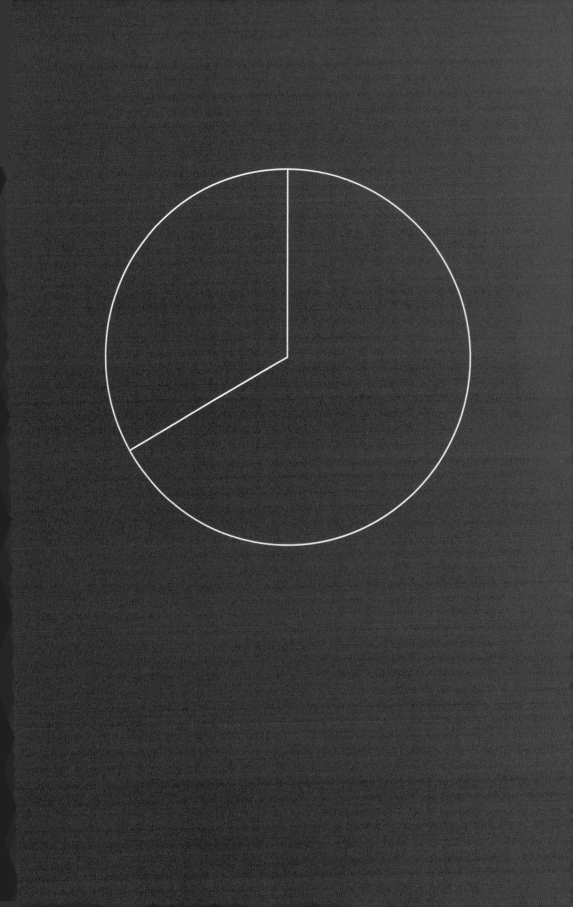

EXPLORATION

10   Conflict domains

ESSENCE   Life is not what it seems to be. This fact is expressed through the Conflict Domains model, which presents four domains where conflict may take place, and which are defined by the relationship between those involved:

o   family and relatives
o   living and environment domain
o   labor and financial domain
o   free choices domain.

Conflicts may arise in a particular environment: the *family* domain, the (living) *environmental* domain, at work or in the *labor* domain, and in a *leisure* environment, such as a network of friends or a sport or hobby club. People partly derive their identity from such domains. Thus the 'domain' influences the parties' perception and interaction and hence the mediation process. The model is useful for the preparation of the intake or exploration phases. The mediator can use this model to assess the focus and the context of the conflict with the parties involved. The model also has a link with *Cloke's cup* (model 50). A conflict at the workplace may be resolved, but the underlying layers need to be reached in order to achieve true solutions and/or reconciliation.

EXPERIENCE   We have used this model for analyzing relationships between parties. Often their relationship is more complex than it seems at first. For instance, we remember a labor dispute where the bookkeeper and the director were in conflict. However, during mediation it became clear they had once been lovers. Moreover, because the director had used his former lover's garden for constructing an (illegal) storehouse, it was a conflict in the living/environmental domain. Also, because of the illegal storehouse, she was blackmailing him. However, he was blackmailing her as well, as she had a Nigerian boyfriend living in the Netherlands illegally. So all domains were relevant here. Such an entangled conflict needs a careful process design (model 9). The mediator should be alert for 'clues' in the words the participants are using, such as the ones described above. These are the entries to the discovery of other domains in the participants' lives that have been affected by the conflict.

EXPLORE   Thiebout, M., K. van Oyen, L.J. Reijerkerk and J.A. Th.M. de Waart. *Groepsmediation: Dynamiek, procesontwerp en werkvormen.* The Hague: SDU Publishers, 2nd edition, 2015.

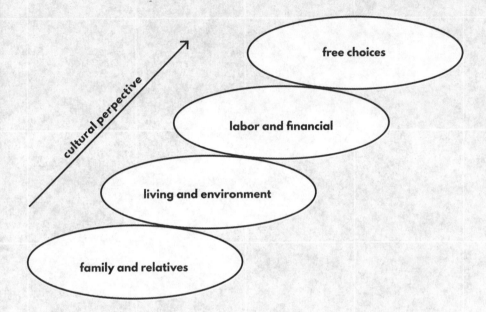

free choices

labor and financial

living and environment

family and relatives

cultural perpective

11   Seven Insights into conflicts

ESSENCE   A conflict has been going on for a while, and you can't see the wood for the trees. Recognize the feeling? The 7-I model will help you better understand the conflict. By asking all seven I-questions, you'll discover the most appropriate intervention:

o   **Individuals** – Who are the conflicting parties? What are their conflict styles? What is their motivation?
o   **Issues** – What is the quarrel about? What are their viewpoints and interests?
o   **Interdependence** – What relationship do parties have? To what extent are they interdependent? What interest do they have in common?
o   **Interaction** – How do parties react to each other? What behavior changes are viable?
o   **Implications** – What is the conflict resulting in? What are the costs and benefits to either, and how can those be influenced?
o   **Institutions** – What is the organizational/relational context of the conflict? What is the conflict culture? Who else is looking on? What characterizes them? What can be changed in this context?
o   **Interventions** – What intervention and which approach are appropriate here? Who else in the entourage can contribute?

EXPERIENCE   Often we have hypotheses about these I's before even the first interview. As long as we realize we have hypotheses and not truths, these assumptions are useful, helping us ask (open) questions. So, use the model as a checklist for yourself or the parties in conflict. To get things going, ask parties to answer these questions on behalf of the other. Imagine Sophia and David having a conflict. Ask Sophia what she thinks are the important issues and interests for David, and how dependent he feels towards her. And what does she thinks impacts most on David in this quarrel? And vice versa with David. Remember to use all Is. You can also ask them to write this down, or you can ask them in caucus. Once familiar with the model, you can ask parties how they think the other will answer a particular question. 'David, what will Sophia answer when asked what the issues are for her?' David: 'Sophia will probably just answer that for her only the children count. While I know she doesn't want me to see Josie, my new girlfriend.' As this gives you information on David's phantasy about Sophia's strategic behavior, you now also have an issue for the agenda.

EXPLORE   Giebels, E. and M.C. Euwema. *Conflictmanagement*. 2nd edition. Groningen/Houten: Noordhoff Uitgevers, 2010.

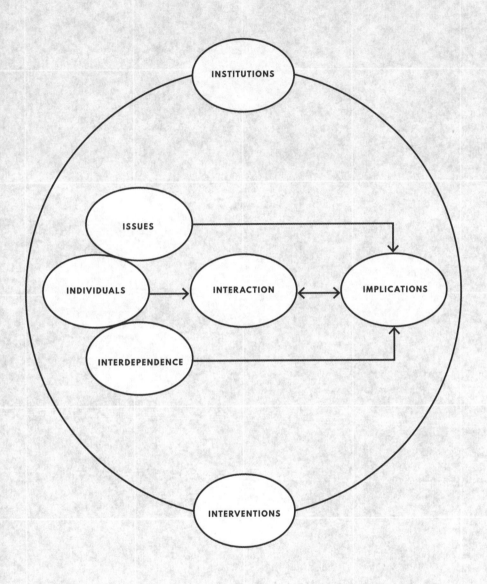

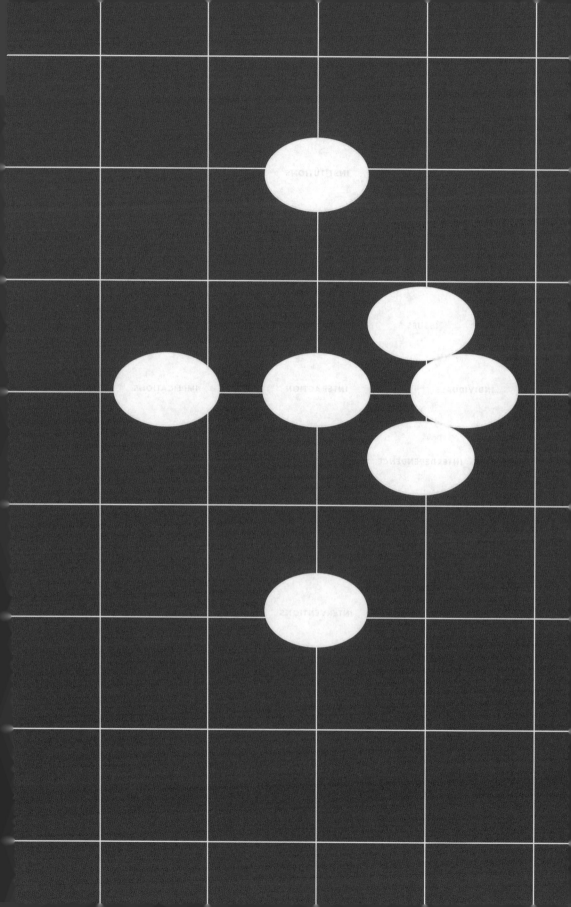

12   Conflict kaleidoscope

ESSENCE   The kaleidoscope model addresses conflict formulation and the way people make sense of the crucial event that has led to the conflict. A person will always choose a perspective in the context of the organization they are working in and the place they occupy there. Secondly, their choice will be determined by the larger social context in which they operate and the result they expect from their choice of perspective. Core questions by the mediator in this model, where the formulation of the conflict is central to making sense of it, are the following. How does someone categorize a certain (crucial) event? In which larger context can the event be situated? And finally, how important does one consider this larger context? The model also distinguishes four perspectives. First is the substantive perspective where the violation of the content of a norm is central. Second comes the relational process perspective where violation of the communication process norm is central. Third, the procedural perspective is concerned with the procedural norm violation. And fourth, the behavioral action perspective focuses on the norm violation concerning specific actions towards each other, including the relevant balance of power aspects.

EXPERIENCE   In our experience, making explicit the various perspectives that have been put forward by parties implicitly, creates understanding for and between them. Take, for example, a manager who from the substantive perspective refers to an employee's unacceptable behavior when he violated the security norms in a chemical plant. The employee, on the other hand, states that he absolutely agrees with the security norms, but that the manager far exceeded his authority by the way he humiliated and suspended him (behavioral action perspective). The HR manager, taking part in the meeting, emphasizes (from the relational process perspective) that parties had been having a communication issue for some time. It helps if, as a mediator, you can recognize and make explicit that all three parties had a point, considering their perspectives and backgrounds. We then often use the intervention in order to use the larger context and make explicit how parties arrived at certain positions in the conflict. As a mediator you are, of course, the expert in this field of distinct perspectives, but with this model your expertise may go even one step further.

EXPLORE   Bouwen, R. and C.W.R. Salipante. 'Een caleidoscoop-model voor conflictformulering'. In *Leren leven met groepen*, 26, 1-22,1987. Burrel, G. and G. Morgan (ed.), *Beyond method: A Study of Organizational Research Strategies*. London: Sage, 1983.

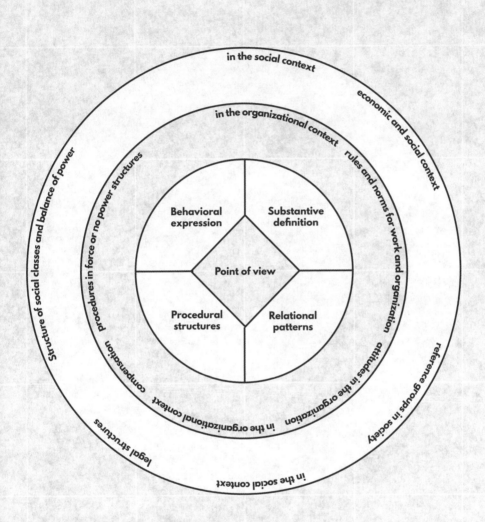

in the social context

economic and social context

in the organizational context

rules and norms for work and organization

Structure of social classes and balance of power

procedures in force or no power structures

Behavioral expression

Substantive definition

Point of view

Procedural structures

Relational patterns

attitudes in the organization

in the organizational context

compensation

legal structures

in the social context

reference groups in society

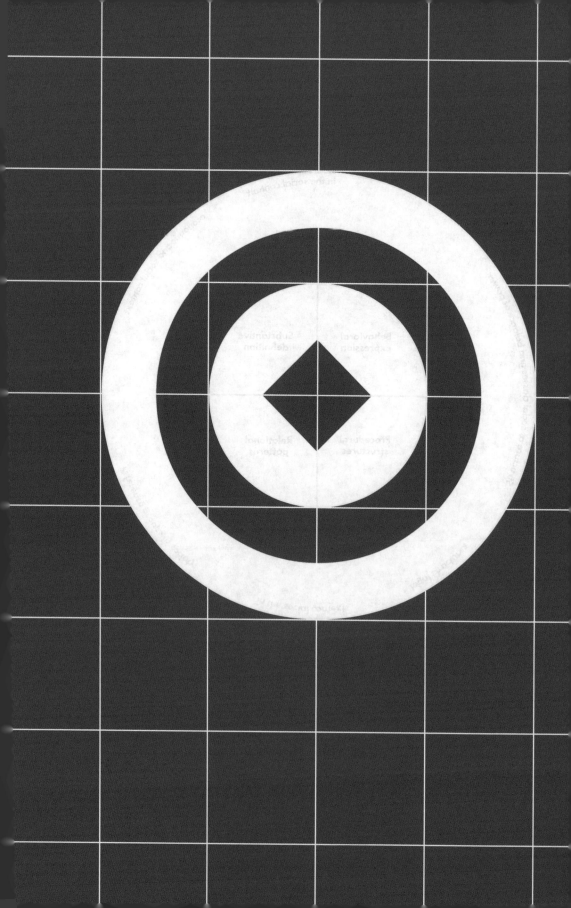

13   Conflict communication patterns

ESSENCE   This model helps you as a mediator to focus on the behavior of the parties in a conflict. It challenges the mediator to step back from the content and to watch from under the eyelashes at what parties are doing to and with each other. How do they keep the quarrel going? And what pattern do you recognize? According to Mac Gillavry you can predict conflict behavior if you base your prediction on the relationship conflict parties have. He distinguishes three kinds of relation, each with its own pattern. Originally he described the patterns in the context of divorce mediation, but they are very appropriate in other kinds of mediation as well. For instance, if parties have a *task-oriented complimentary relation* in which they discuss matters very little, then, in a conflict they will sooner show *compulsive and opting-out behavior*. If parties are in a relationship where they function *autonomously*, a *symmetrical escalation* is more likely to arise. Finally, if parties are accustomed to discuss everything, their behavior in a quarrel will begin to look like *punctuation*. They cannot stop their discussions and the start of every sentence will be punctuated with a 'yes-but'.

EXPERIENCE   We think that recognizing conflict patterns is the core business of mediators. This model is indispensable for our profession because it focuses on the essential contribution a mediator can make to a solution of a conflict, which is breaking through the conflict behavior of parties. By tackling this conflict behavior and the pattern that is demonstrated there, you do something parties can no longer do themselves. Do not succumb to the temptation of pursuing the content of what parties are telling you. That is a trap you do not want to fall into as a mediator because it does not help parties to solve the conflict. So, if the mediation gets stuck and you have the feeling that parties are running around in circles, examine how they talk themselves into a stalemate and put that on the agenda. Act as if the content does not exist and make parties talk about how, together, they maintain their conflict.

EXPLORE   Donald H.D. Mac Gillavry. *Scheidingsbemiddeling*. Houten: Bohn Stafleu Van Loghum, 2012.

What does the relation look like?	What does the behavior look like?	What does the escalation look like?
parallel relation	consultation-oriented behavior	punctuations or 'yes-but' behavior: parties cannot withdraw
symmetrical relation	autonomous behavior	symmetrical escalation
complementary relation	task-oriented behavior	compulsive and opting-out behavior

14 Transactional Analysis

ESSENCE   Transactional analysis (TA) describes how people are structured psychologically. With the ego-state concept (Parent-Adult-Child), TA explains how people function and how they express their personality in their behavior. Humans as social creatures are multi-faceted, changing when in contact with other people. The nature of their transactions is important to understand communication. TA gives insight here, also into the unspoken psychological flow that runs in parallel, depending on which one of three ego-states is used. TA shows what change is needed for more effective communication (reciprocal/complementary adult-adult-transactions), to strengthen the adult. The first ego-state is **parent (exteropsyche)**, in which people behave, feel, and think in response to an unconscious mimicking of how their parents (or parental figures) acted, or to how they interpreted these actions, caring or norming. Second, **adult (neopsyche)** is an ego-state most like a computer, processing information and making predictions without major emotions affecting its operation. In this state, people favor an objective appraisal of reality. Third, **child (archaeopsyche)** is when people behave, feel and think as they did as a child. The child is the source of emotions, creation, recreation, spontaneity and intimacy. There are three kinds of transactions: **reciprocal/complementary** (the simplest), **crossed,** and **ulterior – duplex/angular** (the most complex). Finally, there are four life positions. Holding a particular position has profound implications for how individuals operationalize their lives:

o   I'm not OK, you're OK (I-U+)   o   I'm OK, you're not OK (I+U-)
o   I'm not OK, you're not OK (I-U-)   o   I'm OK, you're OK (I+U+)

EXPERIENCE   People often create pressure in or experience pressure from others to communicate in a way matching their style. For example, a boss talking to his staff as a controlling parent, will engender childlike responses. Employees resisting may be removed or labeled 'trouble'. Transactions can be experienced as positive or negative depending on the nature of the 'strokes' within them. However, a negative transaction is preferred to no transaction at all, because of a fundamental hunger for 'strokes' (see also model 20, *Drama triangle*).

EXPLORE   Karpman, Stephen B. *A Game Free Life: The definitive book on the Drama Triangle and Compassion Triangle by the originator and author*. San Francisco: Drama Triangle Publications 2014. Berne, Eric. *Games People Play*. New York: Ballantine Books, 1996.

person A   # person B

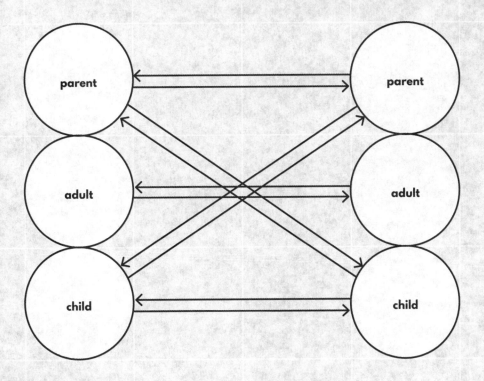

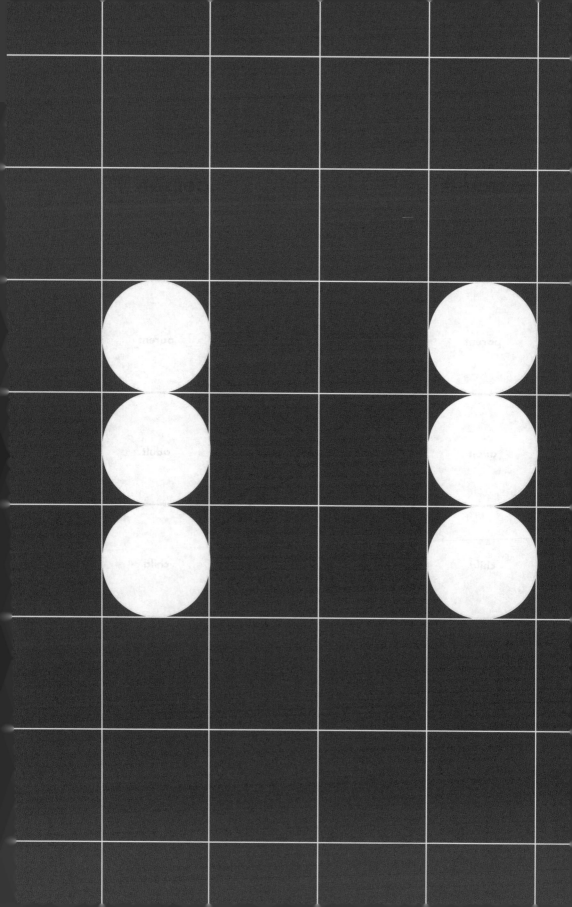

15   Five Wonder Ws

ESSENCE   This meta-communication model consists of 5 questions which regulate communication between mediation participants. These questions must be asked in this particular order:

o What I see you doing is … (description of ineffective communication pattern)
o Will this work ? (awareness-raising question)
o Would you like it to work? (commitment question)
o Why would you like your communication to work? (interest /needs question)
o What could you do or contribute yourself in order to make your communication more effective – to make it work? (solution-focused question)

This tool is mainly used during the exploration phase. By using it, the mediator makes the participants aware of their ineffective communication patterns and gives them a choice to change their repertoire, thus taking responsibility for their behavior. As a result communication may improve remarkably.

EXPERIENCE   This meta-communication model is very effective but needs some ground rules. You should ask all the questions and ask them in the order given above. It is also wise not to use it in too early a stage in the mediation, because participants need to speak out and get rid of their stress and emotions. Therefore, first try other means to regulate participants' communication. If these don't work, then do try the 5 Ws. The mediator can use this model only once. It will sound like a 'trick' if you use this question set twice or more. So, we use it as a last resort, after other meta – communication techniques have failed (see also model 55, *Feedback*). During our training sessions we have noticed that participants often take on the role of a kind of policeman in order to regulate communication: 'You should now be quiet, and allow the other party to have a word, sir'. Not only does this kind of intervention lead to the mediator having to intervene time and again, but it also leads to parties not feeling any responsibility for the way they communicate. The 5 Ws model and comparable meta-communication techniques are much more effective.

EXPLORE   Watzlawick, P., J. Beavin-Bavelas and D. Jackson, *Some Tentative Axioms of Communication in Pragmatics of Human Communication: A Study of Interactional Patterns, Pathologies and Paradoxes*. New York: W. W. Norton, 1967. *CvC Vogelvlucht*, 2012.

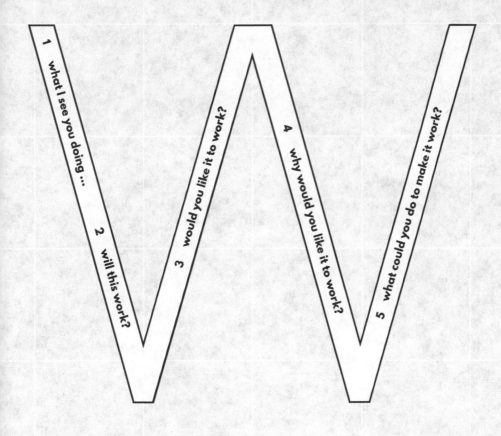

1 what I see you doing ...

2 will this work?

3 would you like it to work?

4 why would you like it to work?

5 what could you do to make it work?

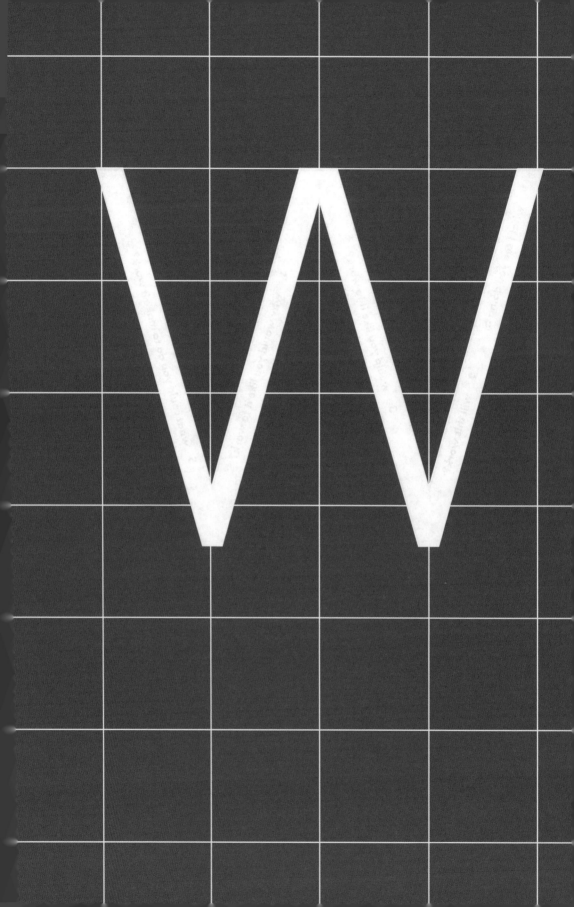

16   Three perceptual positions

ESSENCE   The model of the perceptual positions of NLP describes three perceptions. In the first position you are totally associated with the experience, sensing your body, its tactile awareness and inner sensations. As a mediator it is important to use the information from the first position, and to be alert to your own assumptions, projections, transference and counter-transference. The second position is where you assume the perceptual position of another person, as if you are seeing and hearing the world through their eyes and ears. It gives you recognition and empowerment. Parties need to step out of their first position. The third position or helicopter view is where you step back and take an observer role watching your and others' behavior as if you are outside yourself. It helps see patterns and how parties maintain the conflict. As a mediator you use position shifts to create more space for finding and using effective interventions. You also stimulate parties to use position shifts for behavioral change. Taking different perceptual positions enables you to step out of what you are currently experiencing and to gather new information by seeing things from a different perspective. You can also check how your own words and behavior may be impacting on other people and how they feel. This new knowledge will help you make the necessary changes in your behavior and thus achieve desired outcomes. This is true both for the mediator (self-awareness) and – of course – for the participants.

EXPERIENCE   Conflicts may occur because both parties get sucked into their own perspectives (first position). For effective interventions you need to collect information from all three positions. You could do the following exercise with parties. Create three places on the floor, representing first, second and third position. In caucus, ask parties to step on a different position and talk about what they feel. You can then coach a party through this process. As a result, parties will often communicate differently. As a mediator you will notice that you too have a position you prefer. Varying mediator positions can help get the mediation moving again, if it has got stuck.

EXPLORE   All books about NLP by John Grinder, especially: Dilts, Robert, John Grinder, Richard Bandler, Leslie Cameron-Bandler and Judith Delozier. *Neuro-Linguistic Programming: Volume I: The Study of the Structure of Subjective Experience.* Scotts Valley, CA: Meta Publications, 1980. Grinder, John and Richard Bandler (1983). *Reframing: Neuro-linguistic programming and the transformation of meaning.* Moab, UT: Real People Press, 1983.

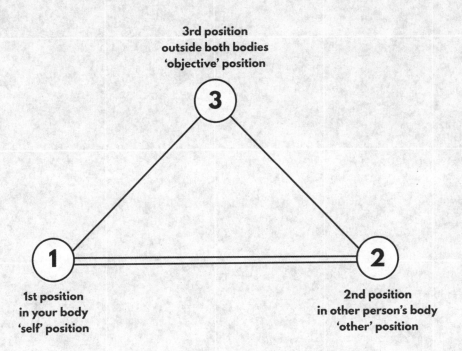

3rd position
outside both bodies
'objective' position

3

1

2

1st position
in your body
'self' position

2nd position
in other person's body
'other' position

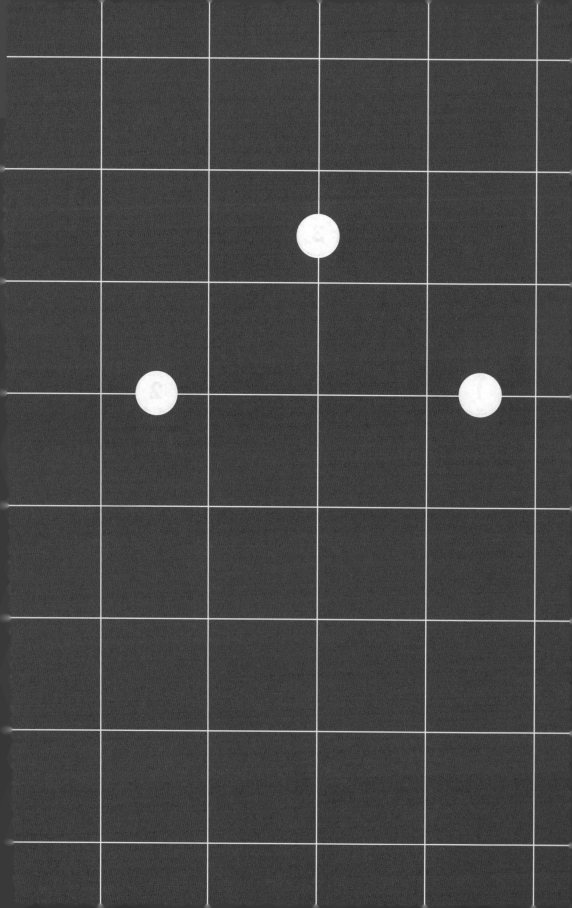

17 Brain structure

ESSENCE Under influence of emotions the limbic system of the brain is activated. This 'reduces' the neocortex where the capacity for rational thinking is situated. No thinking when feeling is there. The limbic system is a complex set of brain structures located on both sides of the thalamus. It is involved in emotion regulation and motivation. The parts of the brain that are part of the limbic system are hippocampus, amygdala, fornix, septum and parts of the thalamus. The model explains (partly) why people behave the way they do when stressed or emotional. They have a problem with thinking rationally. Knowing this, helps the mediator understand that there is a real need to reduce emotions first and get the limbic system less active, while at the same time re-activating rational thinking. Only when people are calm and rational again, is it effective to ask parties to make a deliberate choice. Quite a few mediators don't address emotions at all or hardly, fearing that anger will explode or tears will be shed. But emotions are there. If the mediator neglects them, they will only become bigger' and more explosive (see model 18, *2 Go 4 emotions*).

EXPERIENCE Oh, these emotions! We see parties struggling with their emotions daily. We also see that information is lost and questions are hardly heard and answered, if people are overwhelmed by them. So, during mediation, we give a lot of attention to knowing these emotions when people get 'limbic'. Especially, parties must understand the motives and needs which gave birth to them. Beneath every emotion is a need; which specific need made this person so emotional? What is at stake that it made them shout or cry? We look at them with compassion and professional curiosity. An emotion addressed is a recognized emotion, a first step towards healing. Interestingly, parties sometimes don't even realize what their true needs are. We help them discover and disclose these needs and desires by 'translating' them into needs that can be listened to by the other party (see model 21, *Levels of communication*).

EXPLORE Adams, R.D. and M. Victor. *Principles of Neurology*. New York: MacGraw-Hill, 1985.

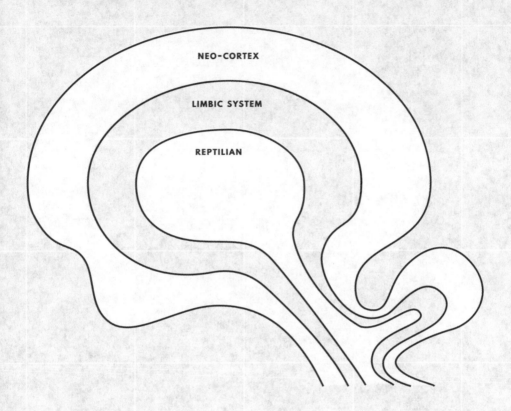

NEO-CORTEX

LIMBIC SYSTEM

REPTILIAN

18   2 go 4 emotions

ESSENCE   The model helps to identify emotions using a framework with four main emotions, happiness, fear, anger and sadness, presented as parts of a pie, and summarized in the memory aid 'glad, bad, mad and sad'. Of course there are scales of intensity in these main categories. For example, anger can vary from light irritation to boiling rage. Sadness varies from being moved, to drowning in a flood of tears. Parties can experience a combination of the main emotions. Jealousy may be a combination of fear of losing, and of anger at being deprived of something. If the mediator uses reflection on feelings as an intervention, that will give room in the discussion to paying examining together how the situation affects each party. Putting a name to a feeling acknowledges it, while ignoring it is counter-productive. If emotions are made explicit, this intervention will help prevent their gaining the upper hand; an emotion named is an emotion subsiding. Particularly if emotions are less visible, this intervention will allow room for experiencing them.

EXPERIENCE   We don't use the model as an image to show to parties but as an instrument for keeping the emotions in mind while facing the participants. Every quarter of the circle stands for a variety of emotions in that quarter. For example, in the 'mad part' we can be irritated, indignant, cross, angry, jealous, vindictive, furious, fucked up and pissed. We should then know how to reflect as adequately as we can. So we use the model to fine-tune this reflection. 'It looks as if you are very much aggrieved and sad. Are you?' There are numerous types of emotions and the more accurate the mediator is when addressing these, the more effective he will be, although it is sometimes difficult to point out the exact emotion. The model also helps mediators to keep an eye open for other emotions not mentioned explicitly. And, of course, it can help the mediator to keep an eye open for his own state of mind during mediation. How am I affected as a mediator by what is happening during the mediation and what emotions are involved there? In the end emotions signal the interests involved. Thinking about emotions is a prelude to investigation of the interests and needs concerned.

EXPLORE   Vries, Manfred Kets de. 'Are You Feeling Mad, Bad, Sad, or Glad?'. In INSEAD *Working Paper Series*. Fontainebleau: INSEAD Global Leadership Centre, 2007.

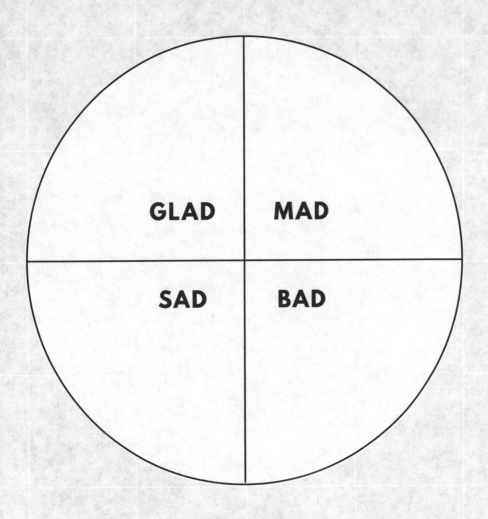

19   Hot-cold conflict behavior

ESSENCE   Different conflict parties will show different conflict behavior. In this model two types are distinguished, cold and warm conflict behavior. With cold behavior the conflict party will say: 'I'm not having a conflict', but in the meantime he will demonstrate behavior with subtly escalating effects. With warm behavior many emotions are shown. We encounter these behaviors in various dynamics, such as:

o   cold – cold conflict behavior; a smoldering fire (igloo)
o   warm – warm conflict behavior; a shower of sparks (volcano)
o   cold – warm conflict behavior; the warm conflict party feels they're talking to a wall.

This model is particularly relevant for mediators dealing with conflicts between citizens and public authorities, and between an individual and a (large) organization. These dynamics are discussed below.

EXPERIENCE   In our experience mediators first must be able to recognize warm and cold conflict behavior. With cold behavior, however, that is sometimes hard. This party will stick to the rules properly and is often quite pleasant. As a mediator you may think 'what a reasonable person' and focus on the other party who should stop being so angry. It is important then to keep wondering what the cold party is doing to make the warm party increasingly angry; and, vice versa, what makes the cold party so icily calm. After all, in a warm-cold conflict we tend to focus on the warm party and ignore the cold party. This re-inforces the dynamics of the conflict behavior and doesn't help parties at all, with the warm party getting hotter and the cold party icier. Therefore do not fall into that trap. It is essential to pay a lot of attention to the cold conflict party, by asking what his worries and wishes are, to reflect carefully on what he is saying and to refer explicitly to the emotions you are hearing between the lines. We sometimes call this heating up the cold conflict party. As mediators we would like to get the conflict, which according to the cold party doesn't exist, discussed. That is how the warm party will cool down and the cold party will heat up, and how the conflict pattern will be broken. The first step to communication between the conflict parties will have been taken, and a solution of the conflict will be getting nearer.

EXPLORE   Allewijn, Dick. *Fair Play on Both Sides: Mediating Disputes between Citizens and Public Authorities*. The Hague: SDU Publishers, 2013.

20　Drama triangle

ESSENCE　The Drama Triangle is a social interaction model describing three roles, the Victim, the Persecutor and the Rescuer, interacting in an unproductive way. Developed by Stephen Karpman, it describes three roles people play in the triangle, and does *not* refer to real victims and persecutors. So there are 1–the person playing the role of *victim*, 2–the person pressurizing, coercing or *persecuting* the victim and 3–the *rescuer*, who intervenes, seemingly desiring to help the situation or the underdog. There is a co-dependency between persecutor, rescuer and victim; without a victim the rescuer has no role to take while to stay a victim, a person needs a rescuer. Also, without a persecutor there is no victim. Karpman stresses the model is dynamic; people may change roles, the rescuer becoming the persecutor or victim and vice versa. This role-switching is a characteristic of the model. He also stresses that the rescue motives are not altruistic but surface motives. Each role has its unspoken selfish needs and wishes, like esteem or acknowledgement. By becoming aware of these roles and deliberately stepping out of them, you can change the pattern. The mediator can initiate this by describing the pattern and making participants aware of the 'game'. The model shows the mediator how participants interact. It may also help mediators to reflect on their own role.

EXPERIENCE　In a child custody mediation some paperwork is required to get Legal Aid for one party. After repeated requests to produce the papers, the mother tells us her house is a mess and she doesn't know where they are. Besides, she says, she has all kinds of problems; her children need special psychiatric attention; she is supervised by a welfare professional, has a case manager, a psychotherapist, an AA contact person, a child protection professional, etc. Neither before nor during sessions does she produce the papers. The co-mediator – wishing to 'rescue' her from this situation – offers to help her organize the mess. The next session again she doesn't produce any documents. The co-mediator 'flips', criticizing her and becoming the persecutor. 'Everybody is against me, even the mediator!', the woman shouts, showing us that the co-mediator had switched roles from rescuer to persecutor, reinforcing the woman's role of victim.

EXPLORE　Karpman, Stephen B. *A Game Free Life: The definitive book on the Drama Triangle and Compassion Triangle by the originator and author*. San Francisco: Drama Triangle Publications 2014. Berne, Eric. *Games People Play*. New York: Ballantine Books, 1996.

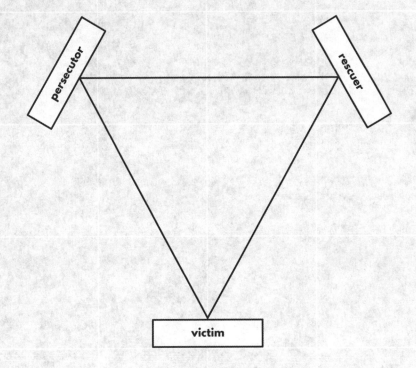

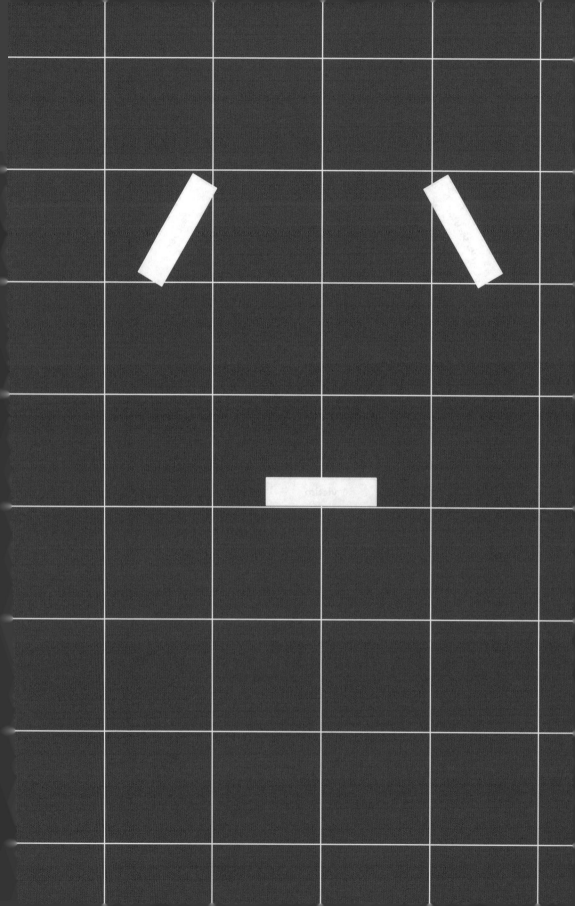

21   Levels of communication

ESSENCE   Levels of Communication is more an intervention than a model as such. It refers to a communication technique designed to reduce emotions, but even more important is the fact that the technique helps to explore needs and motives of participants. One of the features of conflict is that it entails emotions. These may be strong emotions and feelings, but may also be more subtle ones; in a board room, for instance, we often see 'suppressed' emotions, whereas in a family and divorce case strong, dominating emotions present themselves. We regard emotions as a signal for underlying needs (see also 24 for *Hierarchy of needs*). These needs must be met in a mediation in order for participants to be able to move on. Emotion affects rational thinking, and – thus – effective negotiation. Therefore, the mediator must make it easier for the participants to become less emotional and to disclose their true needs. This also contributes to an increased capacity and willingness to negotiate, one of the aims of the exploration phase. The model addresses all levels of the message of a participant:

o   content
o   emotion
o   underlying intention that is beneath the message content.

If used properly, this technique often results in decreased emotions and improved communication. Participants feel they are being heard and listened to and – as a result – they calm down (see model 17, *Brain structure*).

EXPERIENCE   In our experience this is an effective instrument. For instance, in more formal conflicts, such as those involving business or government interests, it looks as if there are no emotions involved. That is when the mediator should be particularly alert to the subtle signals from which those emotions can be deduced (see also model 29 *Iceberg*). By making explicit content, emotion and the underlying need or intention, parties will find it easier to accept each other's point of view. From the start, they will also find it easier to listen to each other. We have experienced that if we use this technique too early it deprives the participant of his 'right' to express his or her grievance or anger. The conflict *has* to be there and must be acknowledged, before it can be mitigated. Should you use this model already during the *Stories* in the *exploration phase*, then it will be less effective.

EXPLORE   CvC Center for Conflict Resolution, *Vogelvlucht*, Haarlem, The Netherlands, 2012.

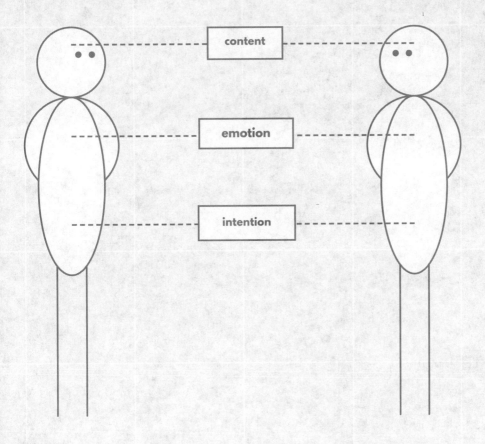

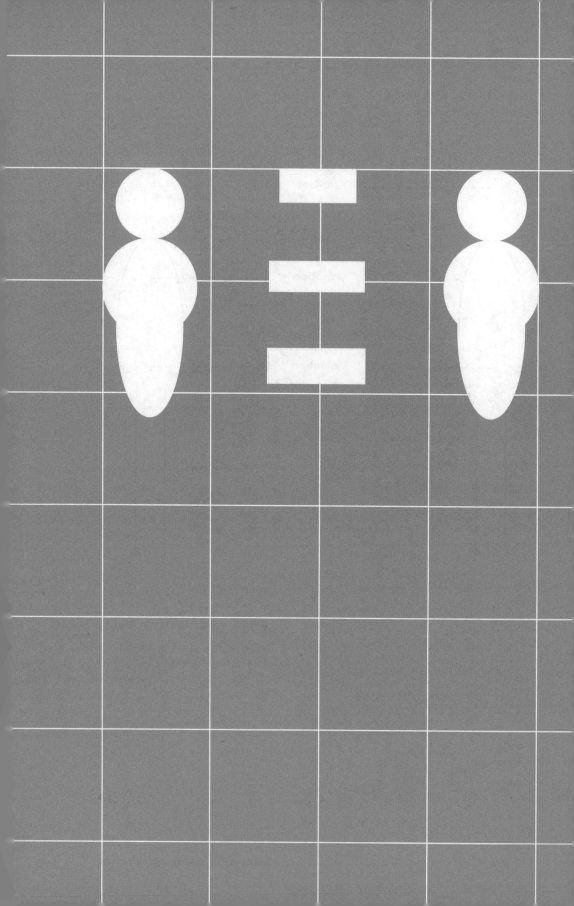

22 ABCDE emotional disturbance

ESSENCE   The essence of this model is that c is not caused by a. By having parties analyze how their beliefs about certain events have Consequences for their behavior and feelings, they can gain new perspectives on their conflict. According to this model people may have a certain belief about an Activating event (A). That Belief (B) makes them feel and act in a certain way: the Consequence (c). By distinguishing the activating event from the belief, a first step is taken. The next step is to Dispute the belief (D). If the belief can be changed, the feelings and behavior will change. Or rather, there will be room for allowing in a new Effective thought (E). The result then is that the interaction between the conflict parties will change.

EXPERIENCE   Our experience has shown us that the ABCDE model is an effective way of engaging conflict parties in a dialogue about their thoughts on critical events (see also model 5, *Stairs of escalation*). These thoughts play an important role in the way one party has come to look at the other party and at the conclusions they draw on the basis of them (intention / invention). The mediator then interviews the participants using the ABCDE model. This can be done in a plenary session but our experience has shown that a caucus is also a good setting for challenging this kind of thoughts and convictions (irrational according to the model) of the parties to the conflict (D). Incidentally, we prefer not to use the term 'irrational thoughts' but prefer to use the more neutral term 'thoughts' or 'convictions' as we assume all cognition to be functional within the historical or situational context of a party to the conflict. In the safe one-to-one setting of a caucus, parties can examine their thoughts and possibly replace them by new more helpful thoughts. Or they can replace them with questions to the other party which can then be asked during the plenary session.

Take note. See to it that the balance is kept. It is easy to be trapped into thinking one of the parties must change his or her beliefs about what happened. We are convinced you need to keep thinking circularly. It takes two to tango!

EXPLORE   See for further reading the many books by Albert Ellis (Albert Ellis Institute, New York), founder of the Rational Emotive Behavior Therapy and the ABCDE model of Emotional Disturbance (e.g. Ellis, 1962 and Ellis, 1977).

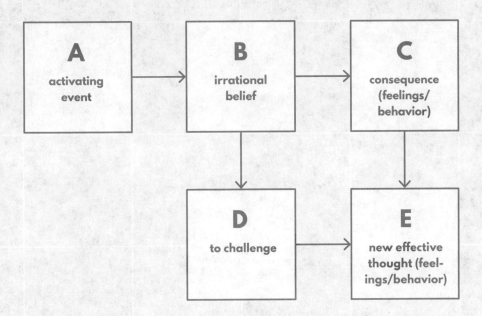

23   Four aspects of a message

ESSENCE   Communication can be difficult. What does a speaker mean? What does the receiver hear? How does their relationship affect communication? Schultz von Thun's model describes the four sides of a message. He developed this model to help us understand the processes of inter-personal exchange. The 4 sides of Schultz von Thun's communication model are:

o   content, factual information
o   relationship
o   expression, self-revelation
o   appeal, request.

The *content* is the factual information. A wife might say to her husband: 'Dear, the garbage bin is full.' The *factual* part of the message is that no more litter can be added. The *relationship* refers to what the sender thinks of the receiver and vice versa. Does the sender respect the other, does he feel friendship? And how does the receiver hear the message; he may, for instance, feel depressed, patronized or accepted. The *expression* or self-revelation refers to the speaker's opinion of the issue, thus revealing something about the speaker's inner world; what are his values, norms or emotions? The message about the bin may be – from an *expression* point of view – that both partners have an equal role to play in household tasks. This expression may be intentional and made consciously, or be made unconsciously (see also model 30, Johari window). The *appeal* side of the message refers to what the sender wants from the receiver. As for the bin, the wife asks her husband to empty it. Awareness of these four aspects of a message gives the mediator a tool to fully understand what parties mean. It also helps parties to clarify their conscious or hidden hopes, requests, values and relationship. It contributes to the process of mediation (see also model 49, *Leary circumplex*).

EXPERIENCE   As mediators we have been trained to understand the message. But sometimes we grope in the dark: the parties have a context in which their communication has evolved and they refer to it. Schultz von Thun's model helps to clarify situations and to get issues transparent. The mediator may ask the wife in the case above: 'Do I understand that it is important for you that there is an equal distribution of tasks and that you actually would like your husband to empty the bin?'. Clarifying these issues contributes to the mediation process.

EXPLORE   F. Schultz von Thun. *Miteinander reden 3-Das 'innere Team' und situationsgerechte Kommunikation*. Reinbek: Rowohlt, 1998.

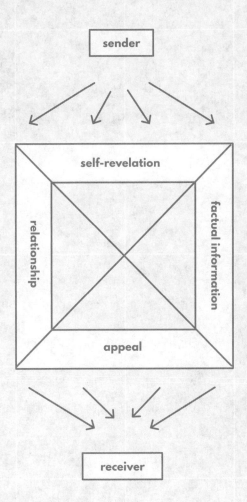

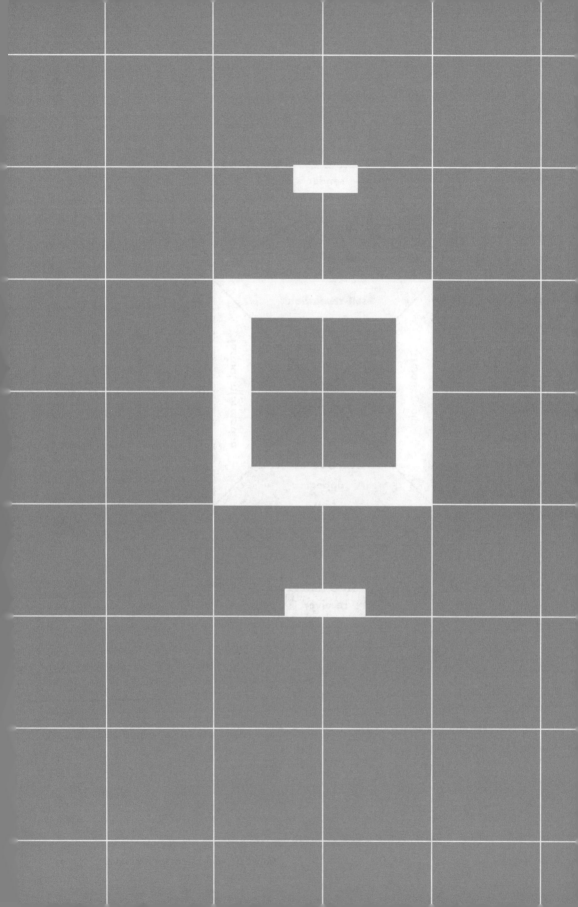

24   Hierarchy of needs

ESSENCE   The model is based on a theory about what drives people. It presupposes universal behavioral drives based on a hierarchy of needs with the most fundamental ones at the bottom. People's higher needs can only be addressed if their lower needs have been met. Or conversely, if the lower needs have not been met, they will need attention first. In mediation this model helps clarify the kind of needs that may be involved in the conflict. On the right-hand you can see the pyramid of needs from bottom to top:

- physiological (food and drink)
- safety (shelter, being secure)
- love and belonging (social network; being accepted as part of the group)
- esteem (being seen as unique)
- self-actualization (trying to be immortal).

EXPERIENCE   The basic assumption that those needs are universal offers opportunities to connect conflict parties. If during mediation the real basic needs of a party have been made clear, this will enable the other party to understand them – as they have the same needs. However, the model cannot be used as a checklist for interviewing the parties. It is a useful tool to keep asking questions, though (*Onion layers of interest*, model 27) until the more fundamental and universal needs have been established. Now, let us assume there is a labor conflict with an employee who has lost his position. The employee may now be demotivated as he cannot develop as he would wish, while the employer is at the same time aiming at terminating the employment as the employee is dysfunctional. This termination of the contract may confront the employee with a drop in income, a serious situation for him as this income is essential to provide for his family. The threat of dismissal may be more prominent than self-actualization. However, both needs can be expressed in the point of view and statement: 'I would like my position back!'.

EXPLORE   Maslow, A.H. 'A Theory of Human Motivation'. *Psychological Review*, 50.4 (1943): 370-396 and http://psychclassics. yorku.ca/Maslow/motivation.htm.

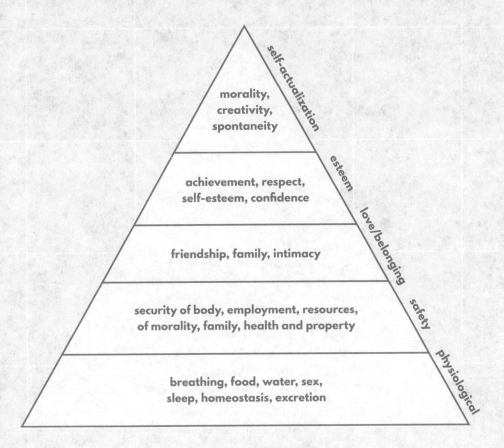

Fairness is what justice really is.   POTTER STEWART

ESSENCE   Interests come in all shapes and sizes. One type of classification makes the important distinction between procedural, psychological and substantive interests. Procedural interests entail wishes and objectives, such as having a voice and being heard, having influence, receiving and giving trust, and finally experiencing a sense of equilibrium. Psychological interests are about cares, needs and fears, such as gaining recognition, getting respect, being appreciated or getting certainty. Substantive interests are motives of content, such as profit, commercial relationships, work or knowing the ins and outs of a situation. For many people procedural interests are a very important if not the most important aspect to people, as is shown in a report by the Netherlands National Ombudsman. After all, everyone wants fair treatment. Psychological interests come second. Substantive interests are addressed thirdly. By re-formulating, reflecting on emotions or by peeling some onion layers, these interests can surface (see models 24 and 27).

EXPERIENCE   Our experience also shows that procedural interests surface first; people want to be heard and have some influence. For instance, in a complaint procedure the words most heard are: 'It's not fair'. Looking for what is, in fact, considered fair, is the next step. The exploration phase is the one where most of these interests are listed. As mediators we know that all three kinds of interests will need to be addressed and put on the flip chart sheet. This model is then a useful memory aid. In a boardroom conflict between 2 members of the board the interests were as follows. One member wanted to be heard; the other thought there should be more trust (procedural interests). Not much later it became apparent that both wanted recognition and appreciation; the one for his contribution to the company's turnover, the other for his vision and strategic contribution. In the end both parties turned out to care about the company's survival and their individual incomes (see models 18, 24 and 27).

EXPLORE   Brenninkmeijer, A.F.M., M. Pel and H.C.M. Prein. *Het belang van belangen: Invalshoeken en visies.* The Hague: SDU, 2007. Tyler, T. R. *Why People Obey the Law.* New Haven CT: Yale University Press, 1990.

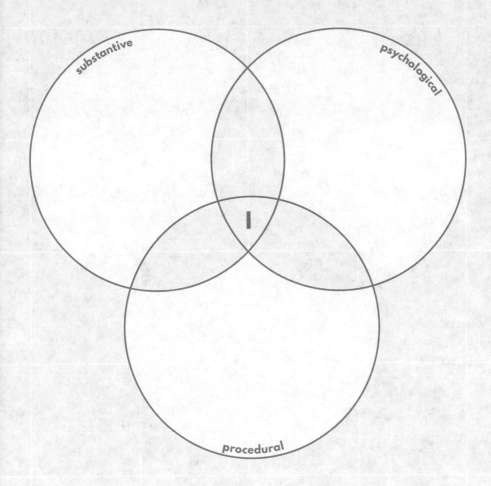

substantive

psychological

I

procedural

26 Positive reframing

ESSENCE   Reframing is a skill that brings a wish or desire out into the open while at the same time mitigating the reproachful message. The Center for Conflict Resolution has developed these questions into a model 'The Effectiveness Bar'. The technique consists of a set of questions ranging from those about the reproaches to those about the anger and anxiety, (see model 18, *2 go 4 emotions*) and then to the sources of anxiety that have led to this blaming or reproaching. The last step is to make the driver, wish or motive explicit. Drivers and motives of the participants are explored in such a way that a clearer picture of what is important to them is established. Participants feel heard and listened to, and emotions decrease. The model helps the mediator to move complaints into wishes, to move parties from past to present and to future, from blaming to embracing, from 'me against you' to 'let's fight the problem together' and 'let's find a solution together'.

EXPERIENCE   This is one of our favorites! We use reframing in all mediations any time when reproaching or laying blame takes place; this will particularly occur during the exploration phase. However, if you use this technique too soon real emotions will be tempered too early. This will deprive participants from empowerment and recognition. Therefore we use it when the conflict stories have unfolded and emotions have come out into the open. There is another interesting phenomenon. When we use this model we notice in general a difference between people; some show sadness, but actually are full of anger; others show anger, but feel grief. In other words, some emotions come first but have a second, – often stronger one – underneath. So, the approach we choose will differ according to the persons participating in the mediation and the first emotion they show.

EXPLORE   Brugge, J. van and M. Schreuder, *Practisch opgelost: mediation als methode voor conflicthantering*. The Hague, SDU, 1997. *CvC Center for Conflict Resolution, Vogelvlucht*, Haarlem, The Netherlands, 2012.

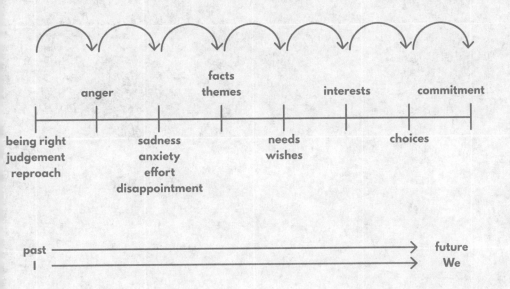

being right
judgement
reproach

anger

sadness
anxiety
effort
disappointment

facts
themes

needs
wishes

interests

choices

commitment

past ——————————————→ future
I ——————————————→ We

27 Onion layers of interests

ESSENCE This model involves an intervention method aimed at discovering underlying interests, in particular if one party sticks to their point of view. The first position is the first onion layer to be unpeeled ('That 2.5m high fence should be demolished.'). This position is often supported by a general conviction or legal norm ('Local regulations allow a height of 2m.'). It entails a general interest ('All neighbors know what's what as regards fences.'). This layer hides more personal interests ('I would like a neighbor who shows me some consideration.' 'I would like an unimpeded view of my surroundings.'). The inner driving force would be 'a secure place of my own'. The model requires the use of 4 specific questions. They help you peel the onion and discover the various layers. Each answer is reframed separately and in a positive way, to show what kind of interests are involved.

- What makes you so convinced?
- Suppose you get what you want, what will that bring you?
- Suppose you don't get what you want, what will be your biggest concern?
- What does this mean to you personally?

EXPERIENCE We regard this model as the queen of interventions and use it in all our mediations. It makes the parties involved move out of any impasse. Parties may have come forward with strong positions, for instance: 'I am entitled to receive at least € 10,000'. Through Peeling the Onion parties realize what the underlying personal needs are and for which interests they can generate alternative options. It is a set of questions leading to insight into parties' interests, from generally formulated positions to deepest personal values and needs. These most personal drives can reconnect parties quite often. The four questions mentioned above need to be put to one party in one session where each answer is reformulated as an interest. Then, preferably, the other party is 'peeled'. Because this method takes time, it needs to be introduced to the parties. A position is a solution chosen by one party. In a conflict these solutions mostly exclude each other (black / white – 'tis / 'tisn't). By returning to the interest that the point of view offers to solve, space is created for more and other solutions.

EXPLORE Brugge, J. van and M. Schreuder, *Practisch opgelost: mediation als methode voor conflicthantering.* The Hague, SDU, 1997. *CvC Center for Conflict Resolution, Vogelvlucht,* Haarlem, The Netherlands, 2012.

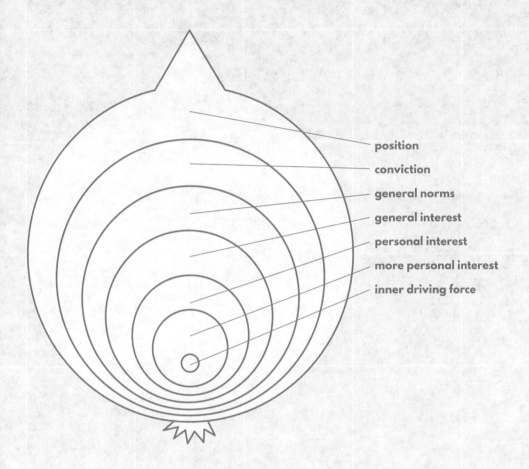

position

conviction

general norms

general interest

personal interest

more personal interest

inner driving force

28   Conflict styles

ESSENCE   In 1974 Kenneth W. Thomas and Ralph H. Kilmann introduced their Thomas–Kilmann Conflict Mode Instrument. Human conflict behavior is determined by many factors. This model shows the relationship between two of these. The focus is on the relationship or on content and/or achieving one's goals. This entails five ways of human behavior when coping with situations of conflicting interests – competing, avoiding, collaborating, accommodating or compromising behavior. The way chosen, consciously or unconsciously, depends on the scale of focus on content and/or relation. The dimensions of *content-focused* and *relation-focused* are also known as the *scale of assertiveness* and the *scale of co-operativeness*, or as *focused on interests of your own* and *focused on the other person's interests*. The mediator can use the model to analyze the relationship between the parties; two parties at the table who both have a more competing conflict style create a different dynamic than parties with an avoiding style. Mediators can then base their interventions on these analyses. The model, however, is not only useful for analyzing behavior between parties. After all, the mediator's style can conflict with the style of one party; the 'avoiding' mediator may be irritated by a party taking a hard line, demanding their rights and showing other competing behavior. Or the other way round. So, the model is also useful for the mediator's self-reflection and choice of role and interventions. The model leads to awareness of what behavior is effective and what is needed for an optimal outcome. You can choose your behavior after careful consideration, aware of the strengths and weaknesses of each style.

EXPERIENCE   We use the model to show parties that the question whether certain behavior is effective, depends on what you would like to achieve. The figure shows how the two dimensions are connected with certain styles, and makes parties aware they have a choice. The most important insight is knowing the incentive for the collaborative approach. That means getting what you really need without forcing (competing) or giving in (accommodating). It also shows the need for communication; if you want the other party to meet your interests, disclosure of underlying needs is essential. On the other hand, if you want the other party to disclose these as well, a safe setting of non-violent questioning is needed.

EXPLORE   Kilmann, Ralph and Kenneth W. Thomas. 'Developing a Forced-Choice Measure of Conflict-Handling Behavior: The 'MODE' Instrument'. In *Educational and Psychological Measurement 37.2 (1977)*: 309.

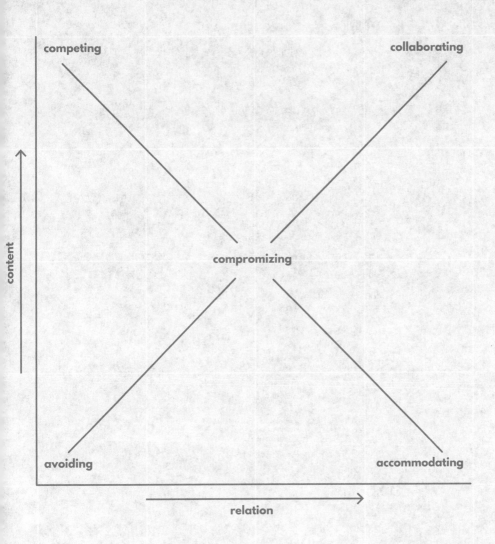

ESSENCE   Positions, emotions, claims and complaints are seen *above* the water surface. Beneath are the real interests, people's needs, motives and longings. A discussion on positions is difficult to resolve, often resulting in a 'yes' or 'no' debate. Interests and needs, however, lay the foundation for a wider range of solutions. The iceberg illustrates this. Since the Titanic disaster we know that the bigger part of an iceberg is underneath the water surface. So it is with conflicts. Positions are put 'on the surface' where emotions and blaming and shaming are present in abundance. As mediators we explore the real issues and turn parties' 'violent communication' into 'non-violent communication', into 'material' that is easier to work with, mainly common interests, but also needs, wishes and desires. This model is linked to the model of *Onion layers of interests* (model 27). The model of the iceberg helps to distinguish between the seen and the unseen; people evoke their position, but

o   behind every position are one or several interests
o   behind every emotion is a need
o   behind every complaint is a desire.

As mediators we want to explore these together with the parties, thus making room for negotiations.

EXPERIENCE   When giving the parties an iceberg each, you notice that the tops never or seldom touch. The bases, however, may over-lap. Apart from their differences, parties have common interests. This is a starting point for the Negotiation or Co-creation Phase (see also model 30, *Johari window*). As experienced mediators we don't consciously use the iceberg anymore: it is an automatically generated concept in our approach. But in our earlier days it helped us distinguish between parties' positions and the 'search' for interests and needs. Was it above or below the waterline what we heard or observed? The 'iceberg' is an ideal way to distinguish between what is seen and heard and what the actual message is (see also model 23, *Four aspects of a message*). It is a useful concept when preparing for the next session (*exploration phase*).

EXPLORE   McClelland, David C. 'Managing motivation to expand human freedom'. *American Psychologist* 33.3 (1978): 201-210.

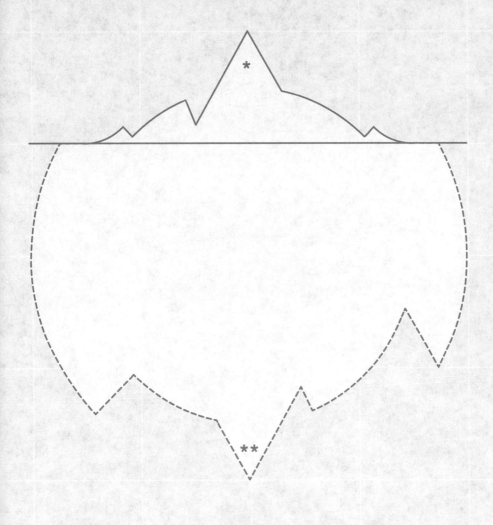

*positions, complaints, emotions
** interests, needs, wishes

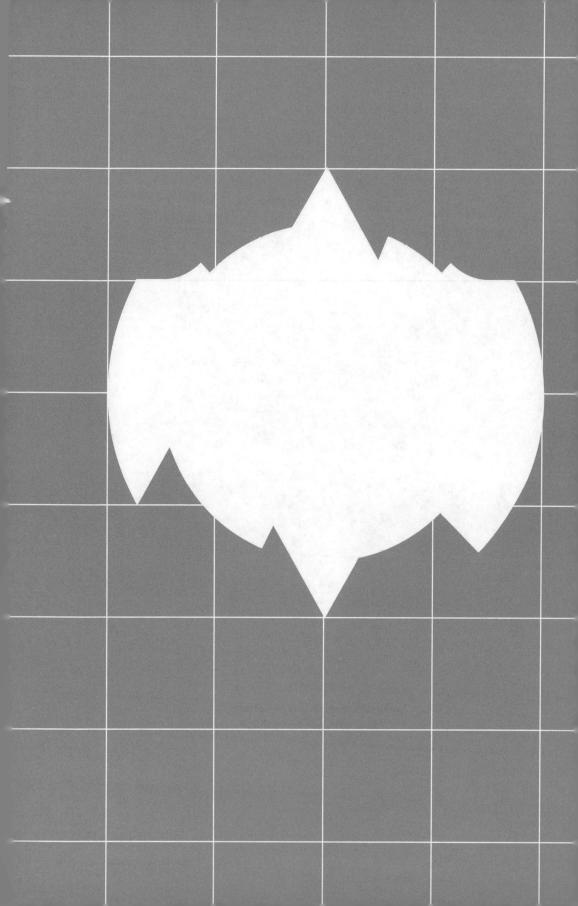

Everyone sees who I appear to be but only a few know the real me. You can only see what I choose to show; there is so much behind this smile. You don't even know.   ANONYMOUS

ESSENCE   The model of the Johari Window helps gain insight into the relations with others and with yourself. It was originally used for self-help groups, among other things to encourage people to give each other feedback. Using four areas (quadrants), this model demonstrates that how you see yourself is different than how others see you. The others see things in you that you don't see yourself (your blind spot). The model also demonstrates that, if you show more of yourself, this can help increase the trust the other person has in you. This will result in others also showing more of themselves. In this way the basis for trust will grow, making it easier to give mutual feedback. By listening to each other's feedback, you can make your own blind spot smaller. Thus you will gain insight into the effect of your behavior on others.

EXPERIENCE   Our experience as mediators is, that by explaining the idea of the Johari Window, you can help participants to understand the value of self-disclosure, and you can encourage them to give and accept constructive feedback. In your role as mediator it is important that you ensure that feedback is given in a constructive way that feels safe for the subjects. This may be prepared in caucus. There are four quadrants in the window. Quadrant 1, *public area*, is the part of ourselves that we see and others see. Quadrant 2, *the blind spot*, contains the aspects that others see but that we are not aware of. It can be very helpful to parties during mediation to hear how the other party has experienced their behavior. This increases insight into their blind spot. With feedback given in a constructive way, this may lead to a new perspective of the interaction between the parties, and possibly to re-adjusting the way they see the other person and – especially the way they see themselves. Quadrant 3, the hidden area is our *private* space, which we ourselves know but keep from others. This is the space that often decreases if trust increases. Quadrant 4, the *unknown* area, is the most mysterious quadrant in that the unconscious or subconscious part of us is seen by neither ourselves nor others.

EXPLORE   The word 'Johari' is taken from the names of Joseph Luft and Harry Ingham, who developed the model in 1955. Luft, J. and H. Ingham. 'The Johari Window: a Graphic Model of Interpersonal Awareness'. *Proceedings of the Western Training Laboratory in Group Development*. Los Angeles: University of California, 1955.

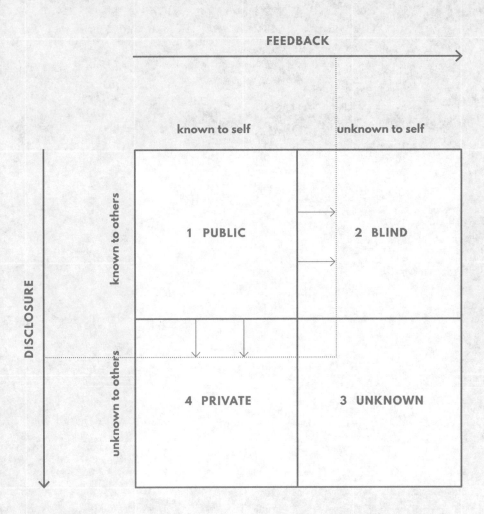

ESSENCE   This model offers a check in order to define whether parties have reached the moment where they can see each other as negotiation partners instead of adversaries. The Transition Phase is a short but very important one. It consists of three questions.

o   Are all conflicting interests on the table?
o   Is there still anything preying on anyone's mind?
o   Are you ready to look for solutions together in your mutual interest?

The first question checks whether all interests are listed, clear and transparent and, in consequence, if the room for negotiation has increased. The second question refers to any emotions; angry or sad people don't negotiate effectively. So, if there still is something bothering anyone, it had better be on the table. Can they, in fact, put their (emotional) differences aside? The last question is to check whether participants are ready for take-off towards true negotiation. Are they willing to look for solutions that benefit all parties? This moment marks the transition of participants; instead of fighting each other they are ready to fight the problem, taking into account their own as well as the other parties' interests.

EXPERIENCE   We use these questions in all our mediations in this particular order, though the way they are formulated may differ. We may use the words more loosely or choose more formal language, depending on the type of client. The questions are a perfect check to assess the mediation process. Do we need to explore more or have all interests been mentioned? Also, have all important emotions been addressed or is there still some grief? We recall a boardroom dispute where all interests had been written on the flip chart, and it *seemed* that all frustrations had been ventilated. However, when checking if there were any emotions left, one of the disputants said yes, but hesitated. The mediator should not miss this non-verbal signal but address it. If he doesn't, the seed for an impasse in the negotiation phase may be sown, there being a need beneath every emotion. That need should not be missed (see model 18 on emotions)! If it appears that one of the participants is not ready, the CvCMediationWheel® allows us to go back and forth until all participants have reached the transition moment.

EXPLORE   Brugge, J. van and M. Schreuder, *Practisch opgelost: mediation als methode voor conflicthantering.* The Hague, SDU, 1997. *CvC Center for Conflict Resolution, Vogelvlucht,* Haarlem, The Netherlands, 2012.

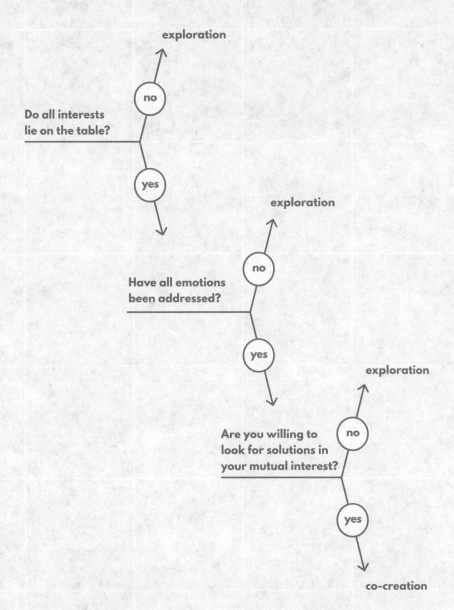

exploration

**Do all interests
lie on the table?**

no

yes

exploration

**Have all emotions
been addressed?**

no

yes

exploration

**Are you willing to
look for solutions in
your mutual interest?**

no

yes

co-creation

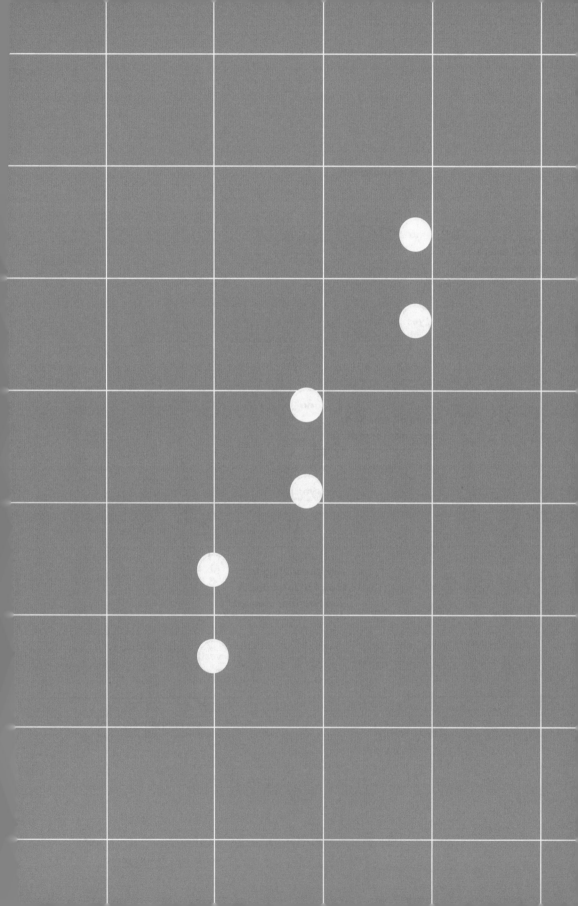

CO-CREATION

ESSENCE The model describes how you prepare for and act actively in negotiations. It has been developed by Fisher and Ury in the Harvard Negotiation Project. It consists of 4 boxes:

- your own needs and interests
- your opponent's needs and interests
- the solutions and contributions you can offer the other party
- the solutions the other party may offer you.

This model helps mediators put forward questions that may give an impulse to the negotiation process. It provides participants with a framework to prepare for the actual negotiation. The effect of using this window is that participants experience a kind of psychological twist; they must really think about a give-and-take and take both perspectives into consideration.

EXPERIENCE We use this model in the negotiation phase to prepare participants for the actual negotiation. In the previous exploration phase the interests have been disclosed and needs have been identified. An interest-based negotiation should then take place. In preparation for the next session we may give participants a piece of paper with the window drawn and their interests and needs listed. Next time they will bring their sheets with the boxes filled in. The mediator invites them to brainstorm their needs, solutions and contributions – preferably in plenary. If participants are still reluctant to come forward with their options, we may ask them in caucus. The Negotiation Window is also useful for group mediation or multi-party cases. For instance, doing separate intakes, we may identify both a party's needs and what they think the needs of the other party are. In plenary they will reveal both their own needs and the opponents' presumed ones. You will be as surprised as they will be! We recall a multiparty mediation regarding the National Water Framework. Six parties were identified, including a group of a 100 citizens who were against the measures proposed by the regional water authority. We interviewed all parties separately during an 'intake caucus' and they filled in the boxes. The most interesting finding was that some parties assumed the interests of some of the other parties but turned out to be 'wrong'. The exchange of the real and the assumed interests was an eye-opener that helped to facilitate the discussion and the negotiation between all parties.

EXPLORE Fisher, Roger, William L. Ury and Bruce Patton. *Getting to Yes: Negotiating Agreement Without Giving In.* New York: Penguin Books, 2011.

My needs and interests	**Their needs and interests**
What can I offer?	**What could they offer?**

Prisoner's dilemma

ESSENCE The prisoner's dilemma illustrates that only a sub-optimum solution is chosen if there is a lack of trust between parties. Of course, trust-building is impossible without the parties being in touch. The model also shows the important role of the mediator influencing the choices parties make, especially if parties don't communicate. An example will show what this means. Two men have committed a crime. They are locked up and interrogated separately. To make the case a statement is needed from either criminal. Now, if both are offered considerable sentence reduction if they inform against their mate, they're faced with the following dilemma. If we both say nothing, we both go free. But if my mate betrays me, I'll be fully punished. If I now inform against my mate sooner than he does against me, I'll be sure to get a shorter sentence. Only if we can both trust each other to keep our mouths shut, is it expedient to keep mum. But how sure can we be?

EXPERIENCE We use this in plenary sessions and in caucus to demonstrate the dilemma that arises if you don't know what the other will do or is willing to do. Sometimes the dilemmas can be presented in a scheme like the one on the right which is used to partialize. The various options can be compared; we can demonstrate what is needed for an optimal choice. It is also a useful model to show the value of mutual trust. Giving an every-day example explains the dilemma: the choice to go by bus or by car during the rush hour. If everybody goes by car, we'll all be stuck in a traffic jam. If we all go by bus, there will be no traffic jam. But then we must all go by bus or it will get stuck in a traffic jam. However, to go by bus I need to go to the bus stop. So my best option is that everybody else goes by bus while I take the car. This is why I go by car. Because everybody else is doing the same, the bus and I both get stuck in a traffic jam. A third party must intervene to break this pattern of behavior, for instance by constructing a car-free bus lane.

EXPLORE Rapoport, A. 'Spread of information through a population with sociostructural bias: I. Assumption of transitivity.' *Bulletin of Mathematical Biophysics* 15 (1953): 523-533.

PRISONER B

	CONFESS	KEEP QUIET
PRISONER A CONFESS	both go to jail for 5 years	prisoner B goes to jail for 10 years prisoner A goes free
KEEP QUIET	prisoner A goes to jail for 10 years prisoner B goes free	both go to jail for 1 year

34 Brainstorming

ESSENCE Brainstorming is a creative method to generate as many new ideas as possible for a particular issue. The creativity for finding many new ideas is sometimes hard to find with (ex-)conflict parties, owing to their having become intransigent during the conflict. Their mind sees only one good solution, and there seems to be no room for other solutions. By the mediator coaching parties during a brainstorm, new solutions, which might be acceptable to those involved in the conflict, are brought up for discussion. With proper brainstorming (see 'Brainstorming rules!' on the next page) you can take advantage of the full experience and creativity of all parties. If one party gets stuck with an idea, another party's creativity and experience can take the idea to the next stage. Of course, you can develop ideas in greater depth with group brainstorming than you can with individual brainstorming.

EXPERIENCE Group brainstorming is often more effective at generating ideas than normal group problem solving. We have experienced that individual brainstorming in caucus is a great way to get a party on the right tack. So, think about having the party brainstorm in caucus, perhaps with the party's lawyer present. After that, you may continue with a group brainstorm with all mediation participants. We believe you often get the best results by combining individual and group brainstorming and by managing the process according to the brainstorm rules. For a brainstorm you can use many creative methods. One that we always like, is asking: 'Who used to be your superhero and which solutions would he have come up with?' It causes an energy surge when people just coming from a sometimes very serious conflict, start talking about Superman, Tarzan, Zorro or Pippi Longstocking. Then as a mediator you ask: 'Think of more options of how your superhero would have solved this situation.' This often generates more ideas, which, as we have often seen, moves parties along. Normally we do not get involved as participants in the brainstorm; it is tricky because it can influence our impartiality as experienced by the parties.

EXPLORE Alex F. Osborn. *How to 'Think Up'*. New York, London: McGraw-Hill Book Co, 1942.

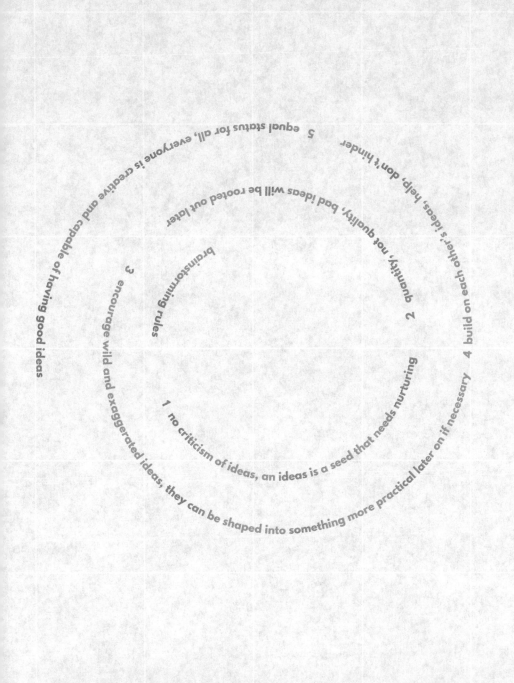

brainstorming rules

1 no criticism of ideas, an ideas is a seed that needs nurturing

2 quantity, not quality, bad ideas will be rooted out later

3 encourage wild and exaggerated ideas, they can be shaped into something more practical later on if necessary

4 build on each other's ideas, help, don't hinder

5 equal status for all, everyone is creative and capable of having good ideas

ESSENCE De Bono's model of Six Thinking Hats® is about stimulating *lateral thinking*, ordering existing information again and differently. For coaches of people in conflict the model can be useful to stimulate parties' lateral thinking. Edward de Bono introduced the term lateral thinking, describing someone whose motto for finding solutions is: 'Suppose it would be possible after all?' This often leads to new and creative insights. The various aspects stimulating lateral thinking can be described thus.

- White hat thinking focuses on data, facts, information known or needed.
- Red hat thinking focuses on feelings, hunches, gut instinct and intuition.
- Yellow hat thinking focuses on values and benefits. Why something may work.
- Black hat thinking focuses on difficulties, potential problems. Why something may not work.
- Green hat thinking focuses on creativity: possibilities, alternatives, solutions, new ideas.
- Blue hat thinking focuses on managing the thinking process, focus, next steps, action plans.

By putting on a specific hat, or more hats, as a conflict party, you look at the problem from various angles. This makes you think differently, which, in its turn, will get the discussion moving and change its nature, creating surprising alternatives and ideas.

EXPERIENCE People tend to approach problems always with the same strategy, particularly in a conflict situation, fiercely dividing along specific lines of conflict. Yet they still have to solve the problems together. If the quarrel has subsided somewhat, then the 'hat' approach is useful for getting parties to find a solution for their issue. Mostly we start with brainstorming, but if that doesn't work, De Bono's Hat model is worth a try. A brainstorm may not work because of parties' inhibiting norms. One party, for instance, thinks one shouldn't say certain things. The other party thinks one can. De Bono's Hats invite people to say anything and everything that needs saying. It's not really *you* saying it; it's the perspective from the hat. This liberates and helps parties to become more creative – which often brings parties closer to a satisfactory solution.

EXPLORE De Bono, Edward. *Six Thinking Hats: An Essential Approach to Business Management*. Boston, Toronto: Little, Brown & Company, 1985.

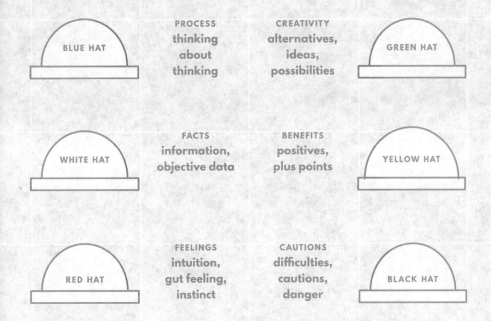

BLUE HAT

PROCESS
thinking
about
thinking

CREATIVITY
alternatives,
ideas,
possibilities

GREEN HAT

WHITE HAT

FACTS
information,
objective data

BENEFITS
positives,
plus points

YELLOW HAT

RED HAT

FEELINGS
intuition,
gut feeling,
instinct

CAUTIONS
difficulties,
cautions,
danger

BLACK HAT

ESSENCE Diverging and converging characterize the mediating process at the start of the negotiation stage. Diverging means having as many ideas generated by parties as they can. It is about broadening the view and looking for all possible alternatives, while deferring judgment. It can be a chaotic process during which you use creative techniques. On the other hand, for converging you coach parties to choose and develop specific ideas so that in the end one has a short list with detailed and useful ideas. This part of the process is about focusing and selecting. Parties in conflict are looking for what would work best for them, and which idea most answers their needs and requirements. Making choices is central to this process.

EXPERIENCE While 'diverging' you can do a regular brainstorm. You will ask conflict parties if they are willing
○ to come up with as many ideas as possible to service all interests on the table; this means also generating ideas that might be in the other party's interests;
○ to defer judgment and not to raise any objections yet, but perhaps build on the other party's ideas; to think out of the box and accept that 'the sky is the limit', thus emphasizing that only at a later stage parties will examine what is useful and feasible.
It is a good idea to have parties brainstorm individually first and then in a plenary. After an ordinary brainstorm we then use creative mental tools. For example, we ask parties who is their superhero and how their superhero would solve this problem. This often alleviates the seriousness of the session and introduces some crazy ideas to the list, which in their turn may lead to more realistic and useful solutions. Parties often have already walked the beaten track. A first converging step may have parties clustering ideas, according to their own classification. Sticky notes on the wall will do the trick. You then have parties assess the ideas on offer with objective criteria and fair procedures … or with criteria like originality and practicality.

EXPLORE Osborn, A.F. *Applied imagination: Principles and procedures of creative problem solving*. 3rd revised edition. New York: Charles Scribner's Sons, 1963. Lehrer, Jonah. 'GROUPTHINK'. *The New Yorker* 30-1-2012. Retrieved October 2013.

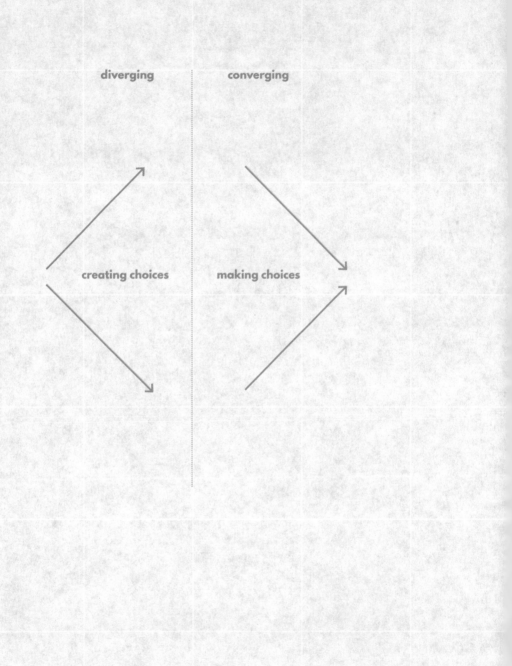

37   Mindmapping

ESSENCE   A mindmap is a diagram made up of concepts, texts, relationships and possibly pictures. These have been arranged in the form of a tree structure around a central theme. The map helps to present complex information intelligibly and comprehensively. It thus greatly helps to structure discussions and brainstorming sessions, and contributes to the organization of information. A mindmap can therefore be used to support creative processes and to learn, to structure and to remember. Mindmapping, however, is not a model as such. Nonetheless, we have decided that mindmapping is worth mentioning as it is such an effective tool in complex mediations. It can be used as a model for the organization of information. We use this tool in the negotiation phase after brainstorming; the different options are clustered and organized in some of the 'branches' of the mindmap. Each 'branch' represents one of the interests. In this way a clear overview of all the options per interest can be observed in one picture.

EXPERIENCE   Mindmapping is a wonderful tool for organizing fuzzy information and clarifying it in this way. We often use the technique when a lot of data present themselves during the exploration phase. Another opportunity presents itself during the negotiation phase when options are brainstormed. Presenting the information through a mindmap gives a clear overview and helps parties when making choices. We recall a multi-party session with a food multinational company. The neighborhood, consisting of approximately 250 people, was worried about their health situation. They also complained, among other things, about dust and noise pollution, lack of external safety and inadequate communication. During the exploration phase more than 150 options had been generated. We presented those in a mindmap in order to keep some track of the suggestions. Using this model certainly contributed to an effective negotiation process.

EXPLORE   Buzan, T. *The Mind Map Book*. New York: Penguin Books, 1991.

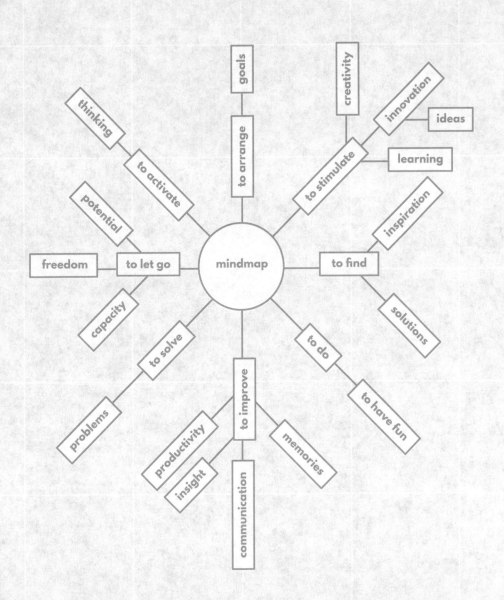

ESSENCE   This model is a matrix for a methodical analysis of the strength of a particular option, most often in connection with the choice of a company or product strategy. The positive and negative aspects are examined using the two external and internal dimensions. Within the organization the question is which strengths and weaknesses can be defined. These are the organizational or product characteristics, specifically only relevant to internal elements. Outside the organization the question is which opportunities and threats can be distinguished for a particular choice. These opportunities and threats concern the external developments, events and influences that impact the organization or the product. SWOT stands for the elements: Strengths, Weaknesses, Opportunities and Threats. The SWOT analysis may be followed by planning questions, in six categories: 1–product (what are we selling?), 2–distribution (how do we get into contact with the customer?), 3–finances (what price should we ask; what costs and investments will be needed?), 4–customer (to whom are we selling?), 5–process (how are we selling?), and 6–management (how do we steer this in the right direction?). After the SWOT analysis the following steps are taken. In the confrontation matrix there is a confrontation of internal and external elements. Issues are defined by *combining internal and external factors* with only the most important ones taken into account. Then the most important issues are turned into *strategic questions*, with the answers to these questions resulting in the *strategy to be followed*.

EXPERIENCE   We use the model in the evaluation of specific solutions. It can also be used for working up specific options. By investigating the four SWOT elements one particular option becomes more specific. It needs mentioning that the method can also be used earlier, in the MediationWheel exploration phase where it can be used for a situation analysis. It is the threats and weaknesses that will have given occasion for mediation. Another version of the SWOT matrix is model 54, the *Tops and tips walls*. In this case the model is used visually and physically as a practical instrument. Parties can walk to either wall or flip chart to give their individual contribution with post-it notes. A plenary evaluation can then take place.

EXPLORE   Stanford Research Institute, Menlo Park (California): Robert F. Stewart, Albert Humphrey, Marion Dosher, Otis Benepe and Birger Lie (1969).

	HELPFUL for your objective	**HARMFUL** for your objective
INTERNAL within organization	**strenghts** _____ _____ _____ _____	**weaknesses** _____ _____ _____ _____
EXTERNAL outside organization	**opportunities** _____ _____ _____ _____	**threats** _____ _____ _____ _____

ESSENCE   Sometimes parties encounter deadlock during the negotiation phase. The *Zone of Possible Agreement* – ZOPA – is a way to establish the potential room for negotiation of the parties. The ZOPA is best discussed during a caucus. It is linked with the BATNA, your *Best Alternative To a Negotiated Agreement* (model 8). In caucus the mediator defines with each party:

o   the minimum 'price' he or she wants to receive
o   the other party's maximum 'price' that he or she wants to pay.

The difference between 1 and 2 is the ZOPA. A price could be a financial price but also a less material one. Establishing the ZOPA may motivate parties to define or reduce the negotiation gap between them. It is our experience that it also may motivate a party to take the last step and reach out to the other.

EXPERIENCE   A landlord and his tenant wanted to resolve their dispute. Notwithstanding the tenancy agreement, they agreed that the tenant would leave the apartment, a beautiful 16th century canal house, for which he would receive payment in return from the landlord. The question was how much. The tenant asked for at least € 50,000, the landlord offering € 20,000. After several interventions neither party came forward with more offers. The mediator decided to go into caucus with the parties and assess the ZOPA. In Caucus the landlord offered € 40,000 maximum, his estimate being that this would cover his costs. The landlord had calculated how much renovation would cost him after the tenant's departure to be able to realize a selling price of the apartment equal to what he had invested. So the ZOPA was € 4,000 – the difference between their two limits.

EXPLORE   Fisher, Roger, William L. Ury and Bruce Patton. *Getting to Yes: Negotiating Agreement Without Giving In.* New York: Penguin Books, 2011.

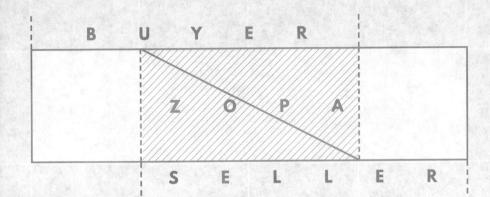

40　Circular questions

ESSENCE　Circular negotiation questions are a question set which may help overcome an impasse in the negotiation phase. Used in this phase only, it consists of 4 questions focusing on what a participant has to offer to and needs from the other party. The order is as follows:

Question to participant A	Question to participant B
○ What do you need from B (1) in order to be ready to accommodate B's interests? (2)	○ What do you need from A in order to be ready to accommodate A's interests?
○ What can you offer B (3) so that B is willing to cater to your interest? (4)	○ What can you offer A so that A is willing to cater to your interest?

First, mention the interests of both parties: *'What is most important for you is…'* Second, questions are always linked. If you change the order, you may encounter the problem of a party feeling he has to give twice, without receiving anything in return. Third, interests of participants differ. Check their reactions carefully. If one party demands €30,000 and in return offers to see their children once a year, it's clear there is no balance (depending on the case, of course). The effects of this tool are as follows. If used when negotiations start slowly, it stimulates the negotiation process. It then helps to overcome final distributive approaches (e.g. both participants want to be the most important parent and both participants want to stay in the family home).
It will encourage participants to think about the other party (special form of relational query) and about the negotiation process (give and take) – although they may also think the questions too complicated. It may help keep the concession burden balanced. Finally, it stimulates commitment to look for opportunities.

EXPERIENCE　Do choose the right questions to start with. Our experience is that first putting the question 'what somebody needs' and then the question 'what somebody may offer', works best. People like thinking about what they need. The questions, however, are complicated to ask and also not easy for participants to understand. Therefore, we often give this brain crusher as 'homework' in order to prepare for the next meeting..

EXPLORE　Brugge, J. van and M. Schreuder, *Practisch opgelost: mediation als methode voor conflicthantering.* The Hague, SDU, 1997. *CvC Center for Conflict Resolution, Vogelvlucht*, Haarlem, The Netherlands, 2012.

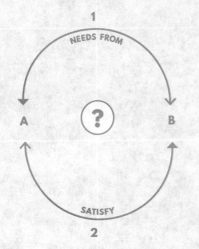

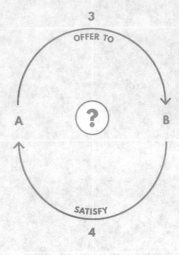

41 Interpartiality

ESSENCE   A mediator's position is special. A mediator is neither *partisan* or *above the parties*, but they occupy the middle ground *between* the parties. They must be neutral and always operate independently and disinterestedly. In a conflict the old adage holds true that the friend of my enemy is my enemy. The mediator should therefore make friends with *both* parties. Promoting a client's interests is a one-sided role. A judge in his judgment or sentence is above the parties. So is someone giving advice. A facilitating mediator therefore takes care not to give advice concerning content. Depending on the mediating style a mediator does not play an advisory or steering role (transformative mediation) or does just that (evaluative mediation). In evaluative mediation the advice should not be biased but be directed towards information needed for the process, such as about rights and duties during a divorce or rescission of an employment contract.
The model on the right-hand may help keep the mediator role in focus always (see model 4, *VISC process choices*). The model keeps the role of the mediator transparent and underlines some of the qualities of the mediator and the mediation process:

o   impartiality
o   party autonomy
o   independence
o   integrity.

A simplified representation of the model can help parties to understand the mediator's role and position.

EXPERIENCE   This model helps to clarify and explain the role of the mediator. In our mediation practice it helps us to clarify our role time and again. It helps mediators themselves to determine whether they are still operating in their role as mediator. It also helps our clients. Especially if participants are in an impasse and are desperately asking for the mediator's advice, the model helps clarify why we do not give any. This model does not belong in a particular phase; the subject may pop up at any time during the process.

EXPLORE   Fisher, Roger, William L. Ury and Bruce Patton. *Getting to Yes: Negotiating Agreement Without Giving In.* New York: Penguin Books, 2011.

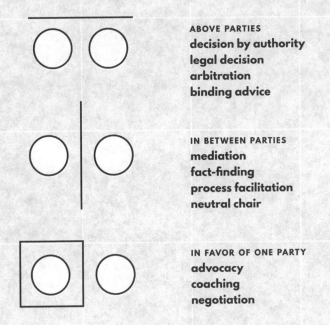

ABOVE PARTIES
decision by authority
legal decision
arbitration
binding advice

IN BETWEEN PARTIES
mediation
fact-finding
process facilitation
neutral chair

IN FAVOR OF ONE PARTY
advocacy
coaching
negotiation

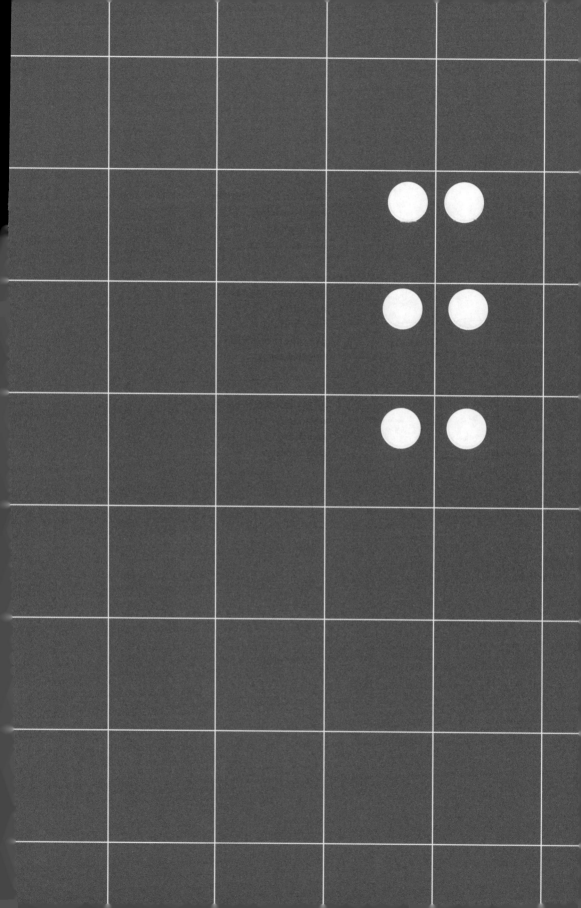

42 Past impasse

ESSENCE   Two children have to share a cake. They agree that each of them would get an equal share. They achieve that by defining a fair procedure. One child will cut the slices and the other will take his part first. In a situation where negotiating parties cannot agree on the *content* of a solution for a specific issue, thus causing an impasse, the mediator can investigate if parties can agree about the *way* a solution could be found. There's one condition; parties should be willing to take each other's positions (interests) into account. This model, being an outline that needs filling in, gives each party room for some brainstorming in order to come up with as many objective criteria and fair procedures as possible, and arrive at an acceptable result. Obviously, some objective criteria might lead to a result favoring one party. Hence the two right-hand columns in the table need to be filled in, to show which result for either party can be predicted for each suggestion made. The next step is to have a plenary session and examine if an objective criterion can be found that does not favor one particular party over the other right from the start.

EXPERIENCE   This method can be used in any kind of conflict. Looking for an objective criterion makes people reflect on the situation, because each party needs to consider what is 'objective' and how that relates to the point at issue – quite often the final point. If parties cannot find the solution themselves, thinking about a fair procedure makes them commit more to finding a common solution. The fair procedure is otherwise often simply an independent expert's judgment, which gives an idea of what BATNA can offer (model 8) but simultaneously makes parties lose control of the results. This exercise leads either to parties embracing a procedure that in the end will create a chance of a definite solution, or makes parties more willing to make concessions and keep control. A sample case. How will you deal with the last gap, to the amount of €5,000.00? One of the options mentioned might be: 'We're going to the Casino and put it on black!' The risk of losing everything makes the other party willing to share the difference.

EXPLORE   Fisher, Roger, William L. Ury and Bruce Patton. *Getting to Yes: Negotiating Agreement Without Giving In.* New York: Penguin Books, 2011.

objective criteria	fair procedures	predictable outcomes for	
		YOU	ME

43   Brink bar

ESSENCE   The model offers four options, going from most to least ideal. It invites parties to reflect on their individual choices using concrete personal images for the various options.

o   **IDEAL** – Imagine it is a Sunday. You are in your garden and the sun is shining. Your favorite drink is within reach. The world is perfect and you come up with the perfect solution for the problem you are having with the other party. That is exactly how you would like it solved. However, there is a slight problem. The other party is enjoying the same sunshine elsewhere and imagining their own ideal solution – chances are, a different one.

o   **DEAL** – It is Monday now and raining. You are being confronted with everyday reality where other people's wishes and needs must be taken into account. You never get it exactly the way you would like it. You must aim at the best possible deal, which will never be ideal and will never meet all needs and wishes.

o   **BATNA** – What if you cannot negotiate a deal? What is then the Best Alternative To a Negotiated Agreement? What is the price of not reaching an agreement?

o   **WATNA** – What if it all goes completely wrong (Worst Alternative To a Negotiated Agreement)? What then?

The model helps the party involved to reflect carefully and make a well-considered choice.

EXPERIENCE   The model is particularly useful if there is an impasse. Use the model as homework for one party while in caucus with the other party; it can also be used in a plenary session. Introduce it with the story you have been reading here. It has been slotted into the 'Drafts' segment of the Wheel because an impasse easily occurs when deals are being made explicit in a document. It is also a useful model for 'Choices'.

EXPLORE   Brink, mr. M. 'Break with the Bar of Brink' (Pauze met de Brinkbalk), *Tijdschrift Conflicthantering*, 2015-5. www. mediate.com.

IDEAL	DEAL	BATNA	WATNA

ESSENCE   The Dynamic Judgment Formation model was formulated by Lex Bos (1974). This lemniscate model focuses on 5 fields: facts / data, concepts / thoughts, questions / emotions, objectives / interests, and means / opportunities. When forming your judgment, you always pass through all these 'fields'. The model shows via which repeating dynamic processes people pass from a problem statement to understanding and judgment (along the *cognitive path*), and to choices and decisions (along the *path of choices*), departing from the following five human features: 1–*feeling* (able to experience and express positive, negative (sympathetic, antipathetic) and ambivalent emotions, right now), 2–*seeing* (able to collect facts, data and history; to remember what happened; to describe circumstances; to give examples), 3–*thinking* (able to conceive notions, points of view, opinions, convictions, norms, reasons, hypotheses or criteria), 4–*desiring* (able to pursue and work towards objectives, ideals, results; to pursue policies; to have ambitions and intentions), 5–*acting* (able to look ahead, look for means and ways to go; to create options; to see opportunities and to choose). These processes occur continuously, both *inside* individuals, *between* individuals, and *between* groups. People forming judgments are continuously and unconsciously switching between levels of content, relationships and interaction. The stimulus for an explicit judgment formation process is the *question*, e.g. 'What does *fair* mean for you in this mediation?'

A central question is a driving force, compass and magnet (Bos). The model demonstrates the 'mine and thine' of the judgment formation process, ordering the chaos of information exchanges, opinions, action-reaction patterns, agendas and preconceived solutions of parties and mediator.

EXPERIENCE   The model can be used in each phase. In the *exploration phase* participants in general focus on past and present, with emphasis on the cognitive process (situations, judgments and prejudices, coping, emotions). The *negotiation phase* is more future-oriented; emphasizing the *path of choices* (needs / objectives / interests and options / opportunities / choices). In the *completion phase* the path of choices leads to discussion and planning ways and means in detail. However, for professional use in actual mediations, mediators do need to practise observation skills during fast changing situations, and develop skills at process, interaction and content levels.

EXPLORE   Bos, A.H. et al. *Forming Judgements: a Path to Inner Freedom*. Randers: Forlaget Ankerhus, 2005.

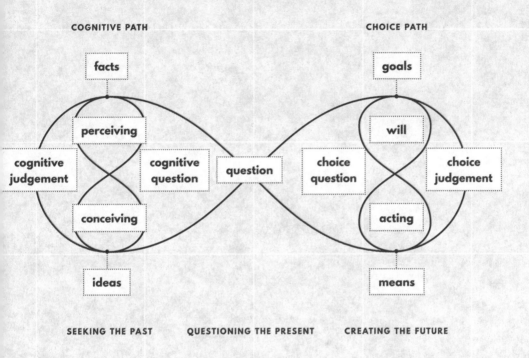

COGNITIVE PATH

CHOICE PATH

facts

goals

perceiving

will

cognitive judgement

cognitive question

question

choice question

choice judgement

conceiving

acting

ideas

means

SEEKING THE PAST   QUESTIONING THE PRESENT   CREATING THE FUTURE

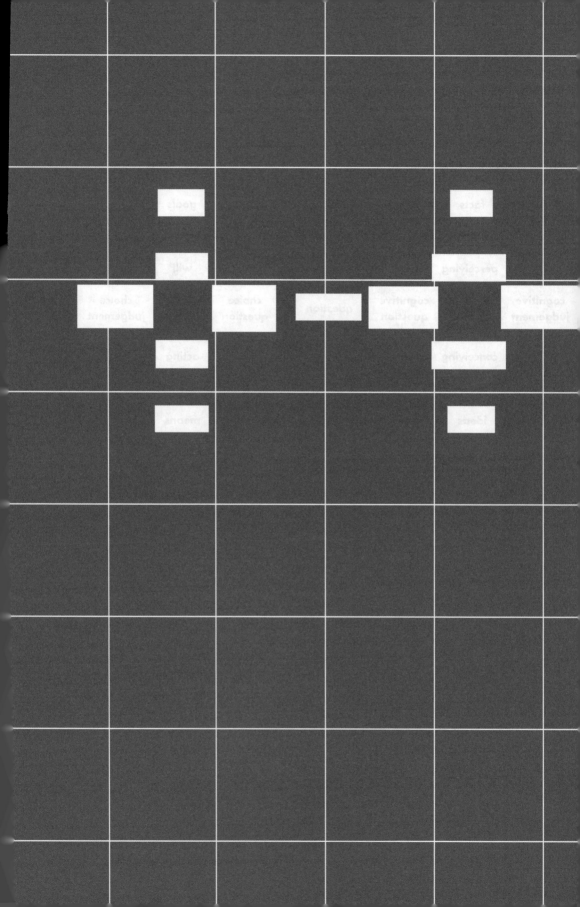

45 SMART

ESSENCE The SMART model gives support in setting feasible objectives. It provides a checklist for realizing achievable goals and solid agreements and for making sure that you pay attention to the various elements of a viable agreement. The word SMART is an abbreviation of the first letters of the next five elements:

o Specific – Do we all have the same understanding of the terms and conditions mentioned; have they been described adequately?

o Measurable – How and with what objective criteria can we measure what we agreed upon?

o Attainable – Is our plan feasible?

o Relevant – Do we solve what we need to solve, or do we need more or something else?

o Time-bound – What timetable can we draw up and agree upon to go through all project stages?

EXPERIENCE Using the model as a list of criteria, check if every part of the potential agreement has been explored sufficiently and if it has been explicitly formulated for all participants before drafting it. It can also be used for individual homework for participants. In particular in the last stage of the mediation process, when parties seem to reach an agreement, it is important to go on asking questions critically and actively. In the euphoria of collective creativity and an improved atmosphere, it is essential that the mediator, as an independent third party, keeps investigating with an open mind. First, what exactly do parties think they are agreeing on? Are they talking about the same thing? Second, questions need to be asked about areas that parties are not aware of yet. If parties in a neighbors' quarrel, for instance, decide to construct a new 2m high fence between their properties, shake hands and are already on their way to the exit, it is up to the mediator to ask where the fence will be exactly, and what length and color, and who will construct it or place the order to have it constructed, and what the deadline is. But 'what if' questions also contribute to a SMART solution, for instance: 'What if one of you decides to move house next month?'.

EXPLORE Roozenburg, Norbert and Johan Eekels. *Productontwerpen, structuur en methoden.* Utrecht: Uitgeverij Lemma, 1998. Uchelen, Iris, S van. *Performancemanagement en resultaatgerichte beloning: een winnend duo voor sturen op resultaten.* On p. 13 Van Uchelen ascribes the term to the British behaviorist Bill Reddin (1930-1999).

ESSENCE   There is nothing better than a good checklist to ensure completeness and accuracy. In particular when drafting an agreement to settle, it is effective to use a checklist for the crucial elements and points of particular interest. The model aims at drawing attention to the importance of a checklist in as early a stage as possible (1st *stage*) when drafting a settlement agreement. The rest of the name is an abbreviation: C-heck, L-ist, A-greement, S-eeking, S-ettlement. In the end one should write one's own optimal checklist, but it is efficient to start with what other people have come up with.

EXPERIENCE   Below you will find a checklist we have found useful for this purpose.
- Who are the appropriate parties: natural persons, legal persons?
- Are they the same as the mediation parties or different?
- Has the identity of the signatories been established?
- Who will sign and for whom is the agreement legally binding?
- Are lawyers or other advisers involved?
- Has the legal advice option been mentioned, also and indeed particularly, if it has been waived?
- Does it concern a referral and has this been included in the considerations?
- Has a complete overview of interests been included in the preamble?
- Does the agreement concern an obligation to perform to the best of one's ability or an obligation to produce a certain result?
- Is the description of all the activities in the agreement sufficiently SMART (model 45)?
- Is the agreement subject to board approval?
- Are warranties included in the agreement?
- Are penalty clauses advisable?
- Is the agreement inside the scope of mediation confidentiality; do parties wish to continue this?
- Is a mediation clause advisable and, if so, included?
- How many copies of the agreement will be made and has this number been included?
- Will the mediator witness the agreement?

EXPLORE   Kennedy, Matthew et al. *WTO Dispute Settlement and the Trips Agreement, Applying Intellectual Property Standards in a Trade Law Framework*. Cambridge University Press & Biztree Inc. Business & legal document Templates, 2016.

1st

C   check

L   list

A   agreement

S   seeking

S   settlement

47   Logical levels

ESSENCE   The way people act and think is linked to what drives them. The model consists of six levels. Every level has a set of questions which help throw light on drivers, motives, worldview and behavior of parties. Dilts and Epstein suggest that there is a hierarchy of qualities which, when aligned, produces personal congruence. Adjustments higher up in the pyramid have more impact.

Logical level	Questions
Vision	What gives me meaning?
Identity	Who? Who am I?
Norms and values	What is important to me? In what am I prepared to invest time, money, energy?
Abilities	What are my abilities? How do I do things?
Behavior	What? What kind of behavior do I show? What do I do?
Context	Where? When?

Logical levels help understand behavior changes from an individual, social or organizational point of view. A change at a higher level is psychologically more complex and has more impact on lower levels. Changes at a lower level may have an impact on higher levels. Changes at a higher level always have an impact on a lower level. Mediators investigate why people do what they do and what drives them. Meaning and vision are essential for a person's way of thinking and acting in a particular situation. Answers help participants understand their own behavior.

EXPERIENCE   When training mediators we stress that their attitude should be in alignment with what they are doing in their work (and daily lives). This will make them more congruent and helps to achieve a 'presence'. For participants, interventions based on this model may lead to a true feeling of choice. They realize where their actions may come from and that they have more than one behavior option as long as they choose in line with their key values. This works best in caucus, less so in plenary. We have used it also in corporate mediations where logical levels form a framework to discuss corporate values and actions.

EXPLORE   Bateson, Gregory. *Steps to an Ecology of Mind.* New York: Ballantine, 1972. Dilts, R.B. and T.A. Epstein. *Dynamic Learning.* California: Meta Publications, 1995.

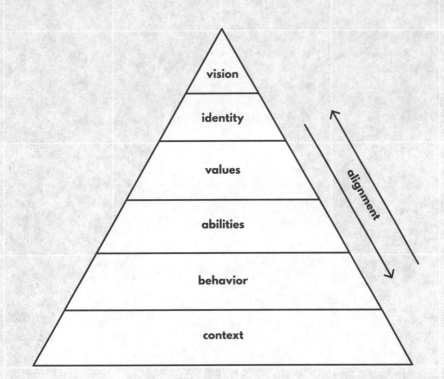

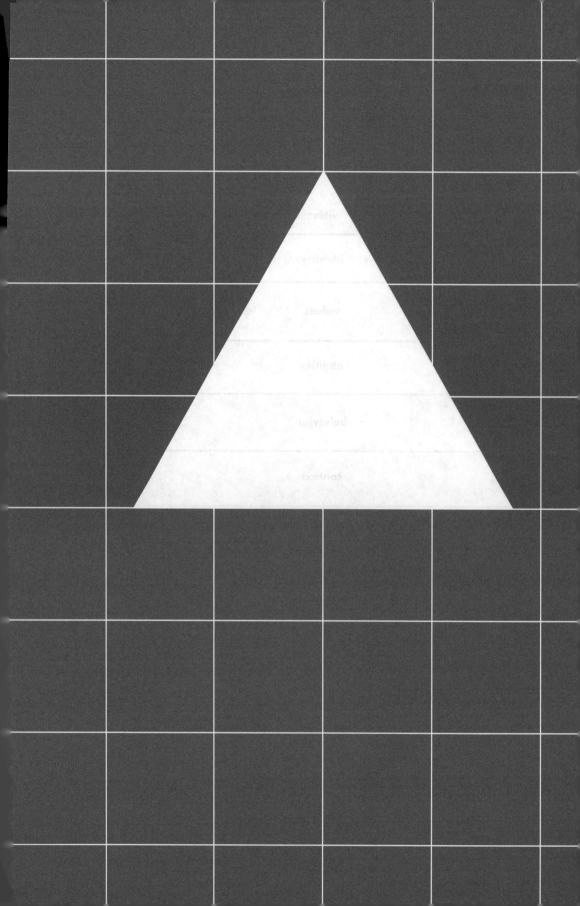

48 Deming circle

ESSENCE The approach of the Deming circle is based on the belief that our knowledge and skills are limited but improving. When parties are reaching a final agreement it is important to emphasize this assumption. The feasibility of a draft settlement agreement is often still doubtful. Awareness helps to prevent parties becoming demoralized if there's still work to be done. With improved knowledge, parties may choose to refine or alter the goal mentioned in their draft settlement agreement. The Deming's PDCA approach can bring them closer to whatever goal they choose. *Plan* means establishing the objectives and processes necessary to deliver results (the settlement agreement) in accordance with the expected output (the interests and goals of the parties). *Do* entails implementing the plan, executing the process, and making the product (the settlement agreement), and collecting data for charting and analysis in the following 'Check' and 'Act' steps. *Check* is for studying the actual results (the agreement) and comparing it with the expected results (fulfillment of the interests). Information is what you need for the next step 'Act'. *Act* is ensuring that parties are achieving what they set out to do and taking action to correct any deficiencies. Deming based his circle on that of Walter A. Shewhart. He called his circle always the Shewhart circle or *PDSA cycle*, where S represents Study.

EXPERIENCE The Deming Circle is a model best used for quality management in the mediation follow-up when some mediators offer parties an evalution session after six months. Besides evaluation questions about how everybody looks back at the mediation process, communication and the relationship, one can also ask questions about the substance of specific agreements reached. For all these questions the Deming circle is appropriate. You can look back with parties at what had been Planned and how that has been Done, to continue with a Check on what effects the implementation had of the interests identified. Then it can be examined if it is possible and indeed desirable to Act to raise the performance level or to formulate additional agreements.

EXPLORE Shewhart, Walter Andrew. *Economic Control of Quality of Manufactured Product / 50th Anniversary Commemorative Issue*, 1980. Deming, W. Edwards. *Out of the Crisis*. MIT Center for Advanced Engineering Study, 1986.

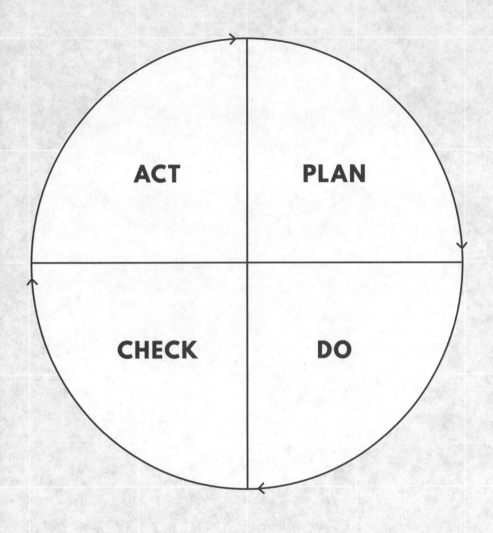

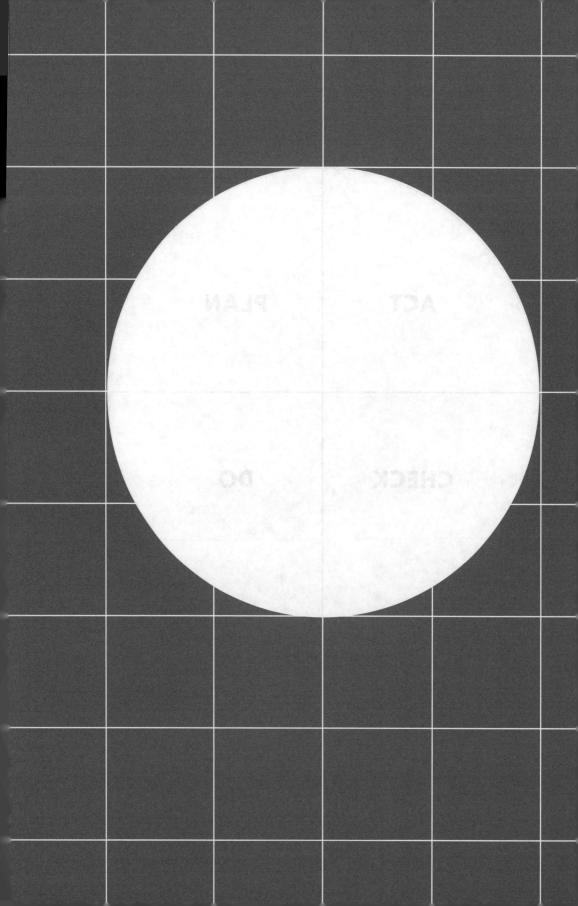

49   Leary circumplex

ESSENCE   This model allows the interaction between parties to be mapped. It gives insight into the hierarchical positions people take during a mediation process. The assumption is that the default reaction we intuitively choose, is not always the most effective one. Becoming aware of this default reaction makes it possible to choose to behave differently, in a more effective way. It can help both mediator and parties to realize that 'together' behavior from one person generally responds into 'together' behavior from the other. 'Opposed' behavior from one person generally elicits new 'opposed' behavior. 'Following' behavior is often answered with 'leading' behavior and vice versa.' 'Leading' behavior is about active and initiating behavior. The other party determines the degree of dominance. 'Following' behavior is about submissive behavior. The individual does not get involved, effaces himself or displays very modest behavior. 'Opposed' behavior is about people who are aggressive and do not agree with other people unquestioningly. They want thorough explanations and motivations before they take action. This could develop into 'defiant' behavior. 'Together' behavior is the ideal situation in which people can work as a team and in which people are receptive to other people's opinions.

EXPERIENCE   We sometimes call the Circumplex the steering wheel of the mediator. The Circumplex supports change of conflict patterns. We have experienced that this model can help in two ways. First, by making us more aware of our attitude as a mediator and of the communication styles during the mediation. What can we do to influence the behavior of parties? Second, by making parties more aware of their interaction with the conflict party. We sometimes use the Circumplex in coaching one party in caucus, making him or her aware of the ineffectiveness of their behavior. It is wonderful to see how enthusiastic some parties become after realizing that they can influence the behavior of the other party by taking responsibility for their own behavior, by following the insights the Circumplex gave them. In this way the Leary Circumplex is part of the 'empowerment and recognition' that is often badly needed to have an effective mediation process.

EXPLORE   Leary, Timothy. *Interpersonal diagnosis of personality: A functional theory and methodology for personality evaluations.* New York: Ronald Press Co, 1957.

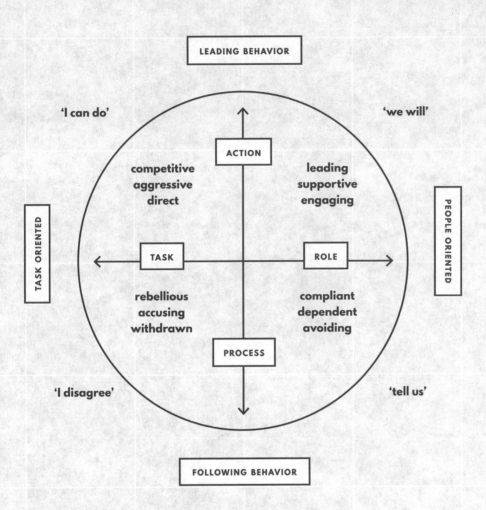

LEADING BEHAVIOR

'I can do'

'we will'

ACTION

competitive
aggressive
direct

leading
supportive
engaging

TASK ORIENTED

PEOPLE ORIENTED

TASK

ROLE

rebellious
accusing
withdrawn

compliant
dependent
avoiding

PROCESS

'I disagree'

'tell us'

FOLLOWING BEHAVIOR

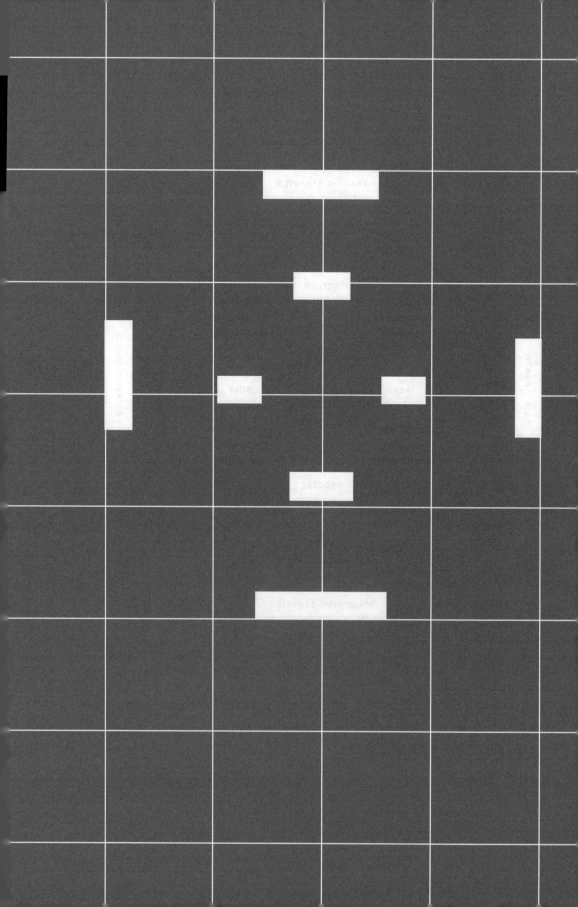

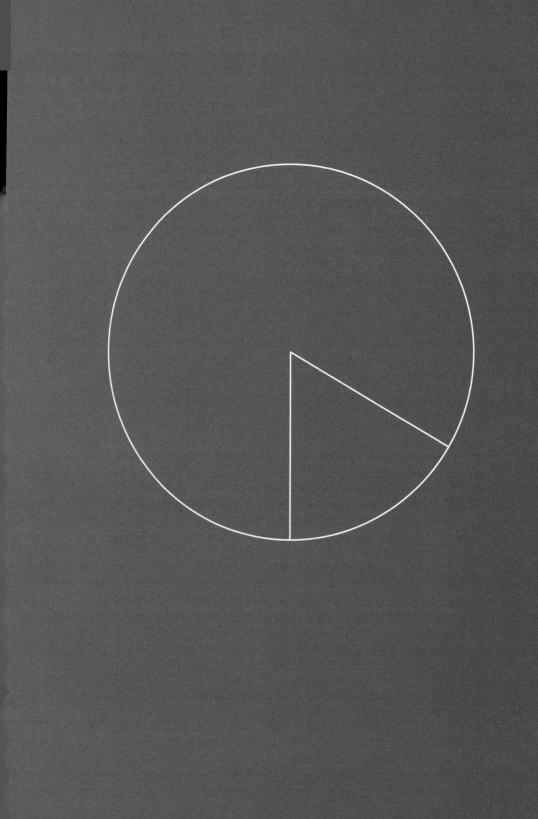

COMPLETION

50   Cloke's cup

ESSENCE   The essence of Kenneth Cloke's model is that a successful mediation takes place at different levels of conflict resolution. The result should be – at least – that the participants stop fighting. Parties conclude their differences are hard to overcome by negotiation or dispute. So they simply stop fighting. The second level is reaching an agreement after participants have negotiated their differences. The third level – solving underlying issues – goes further: a solution is found that covers the participants' interests. Letting go / forgiveness, the fourth level, results in participants leaving the conflict behind them. They can get on with their lives in peace. Reconciliation is at a deeper level. Participants have forgiven each other, and have forgiven themselves. This is achieved at a spiritual level. Few mediations manage this. A change at prevention and systems level is future-oriented and follows the previous level, with the right focus.

EXPERIENCE   We use this model in different ways; first, as an analytical model analyzing what conflict resolution level participants have achieved; secondly, as an intervention instrument during an *impasse* in the negotiation phase, showing participants a copy of Cloke's Cup and asking them what level they would like to achieve. As a result parties start talking about their needs, interests and wishes. Our favorite is the use of the model as an awareness or evaluation instrument. For raising awareness, we ask: 'What do you think you have achieved so far? Would you like to see if you can reach a next level?' The Cup may also be used in combination with 'final questions' at the end of the mediation, e.g. 'How could you improve this result?' It can also be a tool during the closing evaluation phase of the process. Even after signing the final agreement this may result in an extra step / movement / insight. Participants spontaneously say 'sorry', because they realize what their share was in the way their conflict had developed. The level of relationship is related to its use as an intervention instrument. If participants want to continue their relationship it is worth investigating if they need to go deeper into the level of conflict resolution. However, this issue should not be forced (see model 52, *Final question focus*).

EXPLORE   Cloke, Kenneth. *Mediating Dangerously: The Frontiers of Conflict Resolution.* Hoboken, NJ: John Wiley & Sons, 2001.

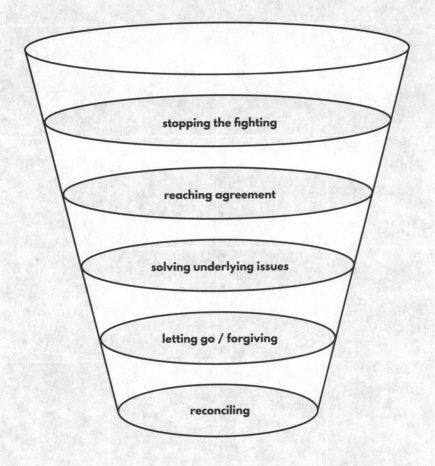

stopping the fighting

reaching agreement

solving underlying issues

letting go / forgiving

reconciling

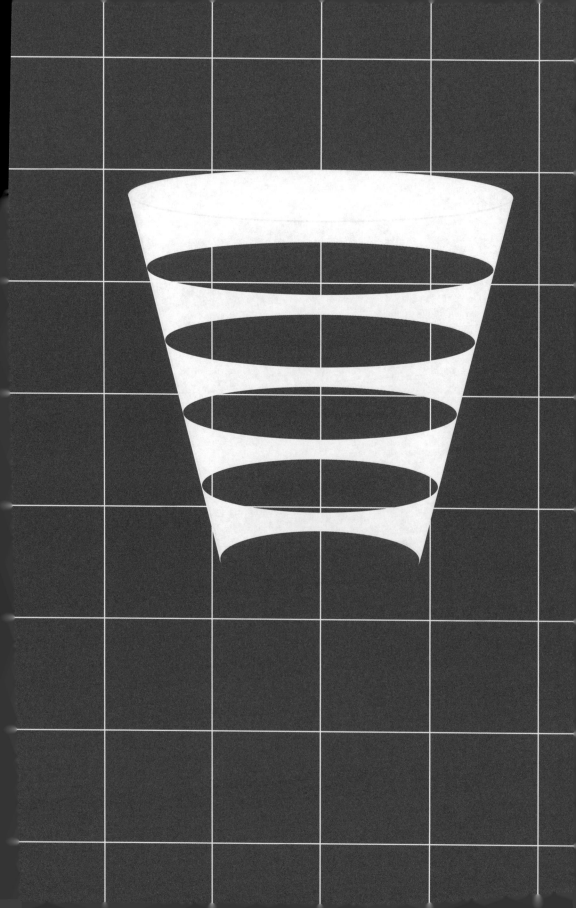

51 Cultural dimensions

ESSENCE   Geert Hofstede was the first to classify cultural differences. In his classification cultures present themselves in 1–symbols and artefacts, 2–traditions, rituals and practices, and 3–values and beliefs. The latter are the core drivers of behavior (see model 47, *Logical levels*). The Nautilus shell (see illustration), with its 3 layers, symbolizes how cultures represent themselves. There are six Cultural Dimensions for values and beliefs among different cultures. Those are: *Power Distance Index, Individualism versus Collectivism, Masculinity versus Femininity, Uncertainty Avoidance Index, Long Term Orientation versus Short Term Orientation*, and *Indulgence versus Restraint*. They give insight into the average pattern of beliefs and values of a culture. Conflicts may arise because of a clash between different values and beliefs. The model therefore helps mediator and participants understand the elements of a culture, which are the (unconscious) guiding principles for behavior and communication.

EXPERIENCE   The model is a tool both in the preparation and process of an intercultural mediation, during the intake as well as the exploration phases, opening our eyes to more or less explicit communication styles and the underlying beliefs. We may notice, for instance, how reputation and face-saving behavior prevails in mediation and prevents open communication or makes showing emotions impossible. In individualist cultures a mediation party can decide for himself, whereas in collectivist cultures often the in-group (extended family) is important for the final result. Sometimes we fill in Hofstede's Intercultural Readiness Check. More often the model gives guidelines for our process design. For instance, we would prefer to have separate intakes to investigate who are the 'significant others' influencing the process and what their role will be in the decision-making process (2 Dimensions: Collectivism versus Individualism, and Power Distance). Or we specifically ask about the importance of the in-group. Because answering these questions may take time, separate intakes are preferred. In plenary, the mediator may then ask strategic questions to highlight relevant issues – with the party's consent, of course.

EXPLORE   Hofstede, G. *Culture's consequences: Comparing values, behaviors, institutions, and organizations across nations*. Thousand Oaks, CA: Sage, 2001. Schelwald-van der Kley, A.J.M. and L.J. Reijerkerk. *Water: A way of life: Sustainable water management in a cultural context.* Leiden: CRC Press, 2009.

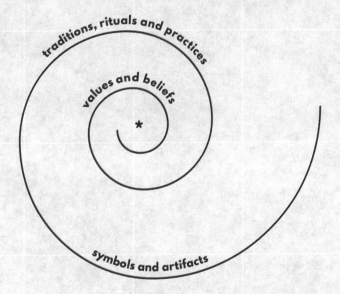

traditions, rituals and practices

values and beliefs

*

symbols and artifacts

* 1 **power distance**
2 **individualism – collectivism**
3 **masculinity – femininity**
4 **uncertainty avoidance**
5 **short term – long-term orientation**
6 **indulgence – restraint**

52 Final question focus

Stop; look; listen. RALPH R. UPTON

ESSENCE This model provides checklists for questioning the parties after the settlement agreement has been signed or after the parties have decided to stop the mediation. It consists of 5 different perspectives to look back and look forward, from the moment the mediation ends. The mediator asks several questions, making each participant focus on

- mediation content
- mediation process
- feedback to the mediator
- own role and growth
- future conflicts.

EXPERIENCE The results of mediation vary from no settlement at all to final reconcialition. *Cloke's cup* (model 50), listing the levels of solving the conflict, helps you to evaluate where parties are. Even mediation without a settlement can be of use to the parties. The final questions help to evaluate the mediation in every aspect and to make participants more aware of the effects of the mediation. As mediators we use the unique moment to get feedback on our role by asking participants their experiences with us as a mediator. What has been the effect of our interventions and attitude? Note that these questions can be asked directly after settlement or after ending the mediation as well as several months later. Realize – as we have experienced - that months later not all parties are willing to look back and answer. Being confronted again with the mediation also means a confrontation with that undesirable situation of conflict, even if all concerned are enthusiastic about the way it has been settled (see model 50, *Cloke's cup*).

EXPLORE Brugge, J. van and M. Schreuder, *Practisch opgelost: mediation als methode voor conflicthantering.* The Hague, SDU, 1997. *CvC Center for Conflict Resolution, Vogelvlucht*, Haarlem, The Netherlands, 2012.

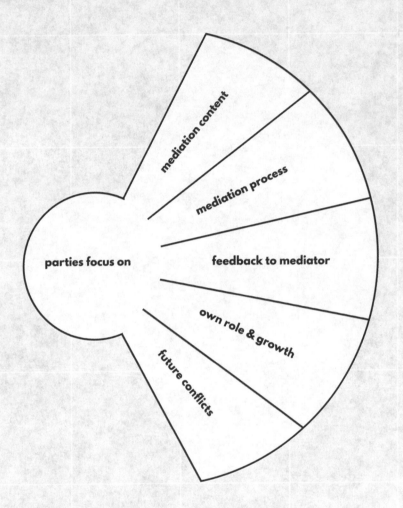

parties focus on

mediation content

mediation process

feedback to mediator

own role & growth

future conflicts

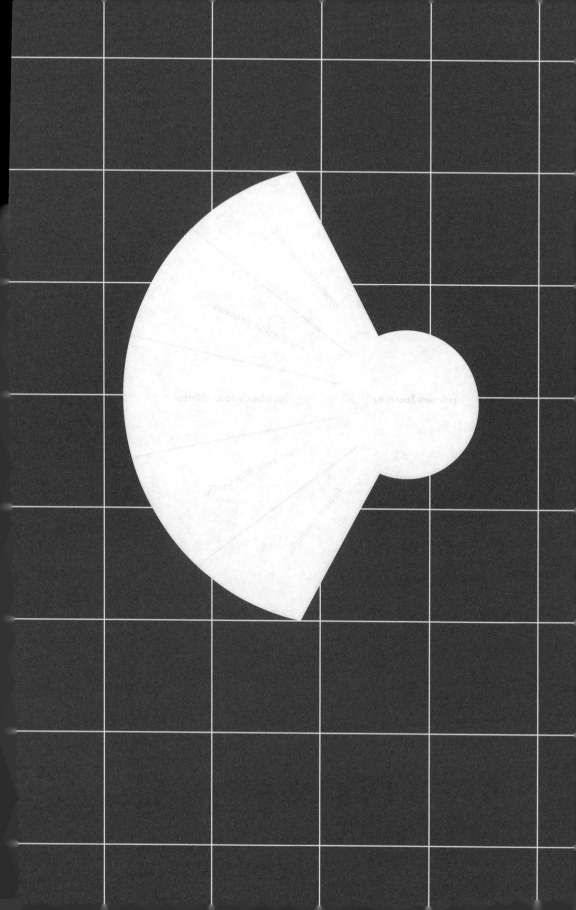

ESSENCE   The Triptych shows participants their transition from past via present to future, which helps them reinforce their positive resources. The left part of the Triptych is the (near) past, the right part the future and in-between you find the resources available for the change. The model was described in *Trance-Formations: Neuro-Linguistic Programming and the Structure of Hypnosis*, and is often used in Neurolinguistic Programming (NLP). We use this model as an amuse-bouche in the final phase by starting the discussion with a question on how participants look back on the conflict period and how their role contributed towards the conflict. Our second question is about the present situation and the third question refers to what they have learned from this process with regard to potential future conflicts and how they will use this knowledge and their new resources in that future. Thus the model might contribute to reach Ken Cloke's deepest level of conflict resolution, which is *systems design*. The effect may be a deeper understanding of their own role and a more future-oriented change in behavior (see also model 50, *Cloke's cup*). It makes participants aware of the transition they have gone through and sustains this movement forward.

EXPERIENCE   This model is great to use in the last mediation phase, the *Completion*. The settlement agreement has been signed and evaluative remarks can be made. When using this model we often notice that participants make an extra move towards each other, apologizing, taking responsibility and reflecting on their own communication styles in the conflict dynamics. For instance, we heard one participant reflect: 'I used to be very critical about her, not saying what I needed, but what I was angry about. In this mediation I've learned to focus on what I need, and also to ask her what she needs. Although it's difficult, I'll try to practise this in future when we talk about what is important for our children'. It may happen then that the other party also reflects on their behavior, which triggers some new emotions of appreciation. This model can also be used in the *exploration phase* (if participants think they can't continue) or in the *negotiation phase* (if participants see no way out).

EXPLORE   Grinder, John and Richard Bandler. *Trance-Formations: Neuro-Linguistic Programming and the Structure of Hypnosis*, Moab, UT: Real People Press, 1981.

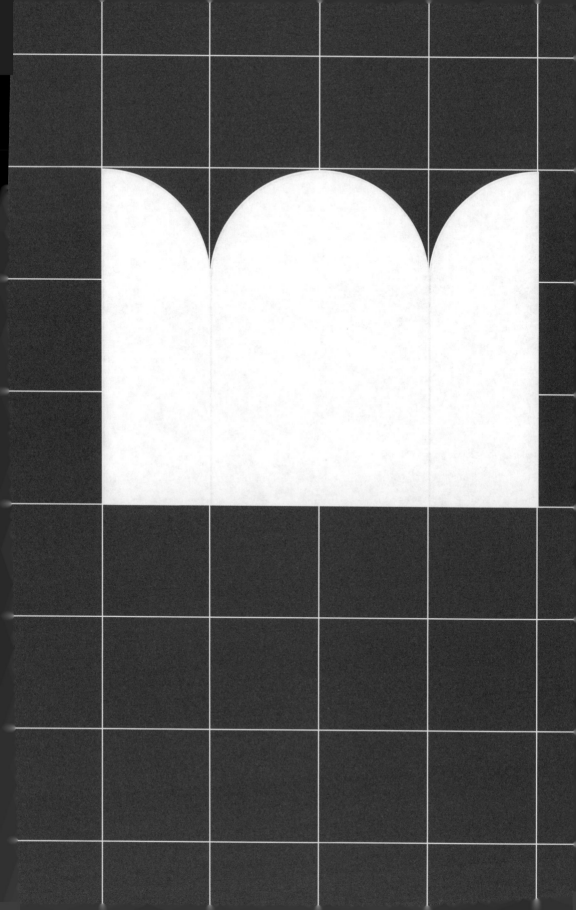

54   Tops and tips wall

ESSENCE   The Tops and Tips wall – also known as Wall of Compliments and Complaints – is a playful and valuable intervention model that creates the opportunity for the participants to come forward with their positive and negative evaluation remarks. As such it is a group activity for collecting individual feedback. The mediator, using two flip chart sheets, gives each of these a heading; one is The Wall of Tops (or compliments); the other is the Wall of Tips (or complaints). Each participant receives at least 5 green and 5 red post-its and writes down just one compliment (green) or one complaint (red) per post-it. When finished, all the post-its can be put on the appropriate wall by the participants or the mediator. The next step is a plenary inventory of all post-its. Can they be organized around themes? The result needs a follow-up. What will be the next step? The result of this model is a collective visualization of individual evaluative remarks and perceptions. As a result a shared evaluation unfolds, a picture of what 'the group' would like to change or would like to keep. Furthermore, by dividing the post-its into pros and cons the model seduces participants to come up with positive elements as well. In general the impact is that participants become more committed to the mediation process. Even if they only have complaints, the wall demands an active contribution.

EXPERIENCE   This model can be used as an evaluative instrument at the end of each session or only once at the end of the mediation process. However, we also use it in the first part of the *exploration phase*; participants are asked what they like and don't like about past events that brought them there. The mediator should be aware that this must be done in a safe and non-aggressive way. That's why sometimes 'Tips' is used instead of 'Complaints'. Decide whether you prefer a limited number of post-its or as many as possible. If the latter, provide more post-its. As an evaluation method the follow-up can be organized, focusing on, for example, behavior, attitude, skills, or process, showing what to continue and what to stop with. Another follow-up is to ask what each person's commitment and contribution will be to achieving the changes desired.

EXPLORE   Berge, A.P. van den, L.J. Boer and J.W. Klootwijk, *Werkboek Werkconferenties*. Vakmedianet Government B.V., April 2015.

Why is it that when one man builds a wall, the next man immediately needs to know what's on the other side?

GEORGE R.R. MARTIN, A GAME OF THRONES

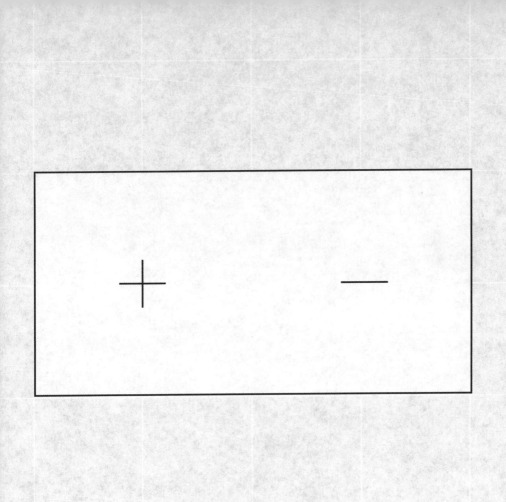

55 Feedback

ESSENCE   Feedback in psychology represents information communicated to someone that is intended to modify their thinking or behavior for the purpose of improving personal learning.

EXPERIENCE   As a mediator you can use feedback in various ways. You can give feedback to individual parties. Most of the time we do this in caucus. You can also coach parties in giving mutual feedback. Perhaps they have tried to behave in a certain manner, based on objectives, expectations and their perceptions. Was this behavior effective? And what were the consequences of this particular behavior on the other participants in the mediation? Of course, mediators cannot answer these questions, but they can give feedback coaching. In the literature many ways to give feedback can be found. We ourselves stick to the following guidelines. Describe concrete observations; stick to the facts and leave your perceptions or interpretations for later. Explain effects on yourself, narrow your description to your feelings, never judge, speak for yourself. Pause and listen for clarifying questions; check if what you have said has been clearly understood. As a mediator you could ask what the participant is trying to accomplish, whether he achieved his goal through his interaction and – if not – whether the participant has an idea about how to be more effective. As a mediator it is important to be perceived as neutral: always keep this in mind when giving feedback to the participants or when supervising the giving and receiving of feedback during mediation. Always be aware that you can use the caucus to give feedback yourself in a safe environment, or to prepare participants in giving feedback to each other. By taking participants into caucus to prepare them for how to give *mutual* feedback, you will ensure an effective plenary session. While preparing in caucus, take the time to clarify parties' feelings and what the role is the other party's behavior plays in this. And then practise giving feedback in caucus.

EXPLORE   Russell, Tim. *Effective Feedback Skills*. London: Kogan Page Limited, 2000.

We all need people who will give us feedback. That's how we improve.

BILL GATES

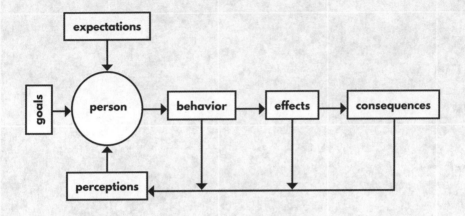

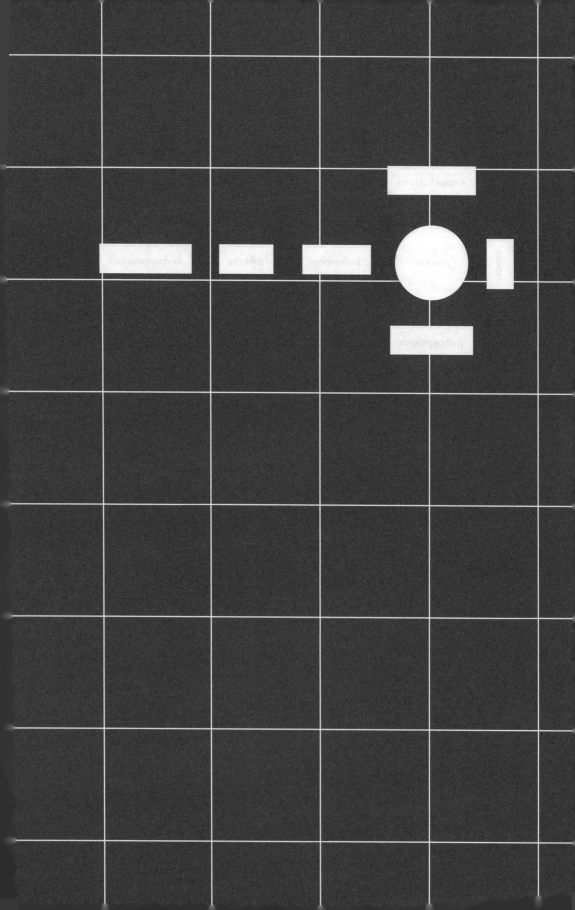

ESSENCE This model was developed by the psychiatrist Elisabeth Kübler-Ross drawing from her experience with terminal patients. She discovered a pattern in the way they coped with their approaching death. She assumed that all people facing loss go through the following stages:

o denial
o anger
o bargaining
o depression
o acceptance.

The stages do not have a fixed order nor does everybody go through all stages. At least two of the stages are experienced by everybody according to Kübler-Ross. Although controversial, the model is still popular. One criticism is that Kübler-Ross does not take the personal environment sufficiently into account. If this is positive, mourning will be experienced differently than if the environment offers negatives.

EXPERIENCE We include this model here to emphasize that mourning and conflict are inextricably bound up. People in conflict often lose something during mediation, such as their hope things will get better again, or the conflict itself. They often feel something is at stake that they risk losing. Or they have lost it already and are fighting for justice. As a mediator it is important to realize when mediation is about loss; this sometimes makes the difference between 'failed' or 'successful' mediation. By discussing this with the parties, a normalizing effect can take place if parties indeed are in mourning during mediation. Our experience is that participants recognize the stages. This makes it easier for parties to talk about loss. It increases understanding of one's own emotions and those of the other people. We also use this model to show that all parties experience loss but are in a different mourning stage. If they recognize this and acknowledge they are all suffering loss, this will often increase understanding and willingness to solve the issue together. Thus this model can improve the relationship.

EXPLORE Kübler-Ross, Elisabeth. E. and David Kessler. *On Grief and Grieving: Finding the Meaning of Grief Through the Five Stages of Loss.* New York: Simon & Schuster Ltd., 2005.

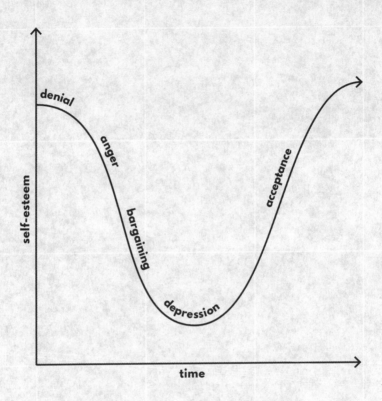

Core quadrant

Straight ahead you can't go very far. ANTOINE DE SAINT-EXUPÉRY

ESSENCE   The model consists of 4 quadrants: your core quality, your pitfall, your challenge and your allergy. It helps you map your qualities and pitfalls. It also helps you see how to become more effective by changing your attitude towards your allergy – your irritation with someone else's behavior, often the behavior you also don't allow yourself. Disapproving, you cannot enjoy the benefits of that behavior. For example, if you hate people being fussy, your pitfall is sloppiness. The quality appreciated by many is that you watch the overall picture well. But you would perhaps be more effective if you also embraced some of this meticulousness in yourself. Your quality of keeping the overall picture in mind would be improved by your operating with greater precision. The person irritating you most is the one you can learn most from. The model is useful to you, when mediating, and useful as a way to make parties understand their conflict dynamics.

EXPERIENCE   We like using this model with parties wishing to understand why their interaction is a problem. By drawing core quadrants, they improve their understanding of how it operates. It can be effective if parties understand that the behavior they are allergic to is precisely the behavior they can learn from and which would make them more effective. The behavior they deplore, is part of who they are themselves. For instance, if you are irritated by your opponent's indecisiveness, you would be more effective if you gave him more room and would allow yourself more time to doubt. It is best to recognize and accept the doubting Thomas in yourself. And vice versa. The doubting Thomas who is in a conflict with someone who likes forcing issues, might judge him more charitably if he embraced this side in himself. With this exercise, the mediator can often break through the quarrelsome behavior and tempt the parties towards a more charitable look at themselves and the other person or persons.

Party 1	*Core quality:* powerful	*Pitfall:* pushy
	Allergy: indecisive	*Challenge:* fussiness, giving room for doubt to improve quality
Party 2	*Core quality:* open	*Pitfall:* continuing mentioning all the options
	Allergy: forcing	*Challenge:* choosing

EXPLORE   Ofman, D. *Core Qualities: A Gateway to Human Resources.* London: Cyan Communications, 2004.

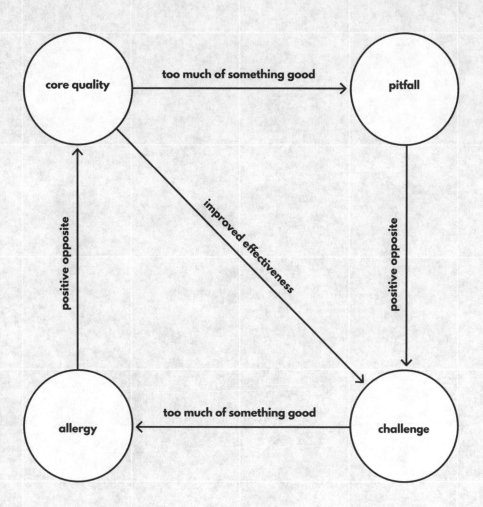

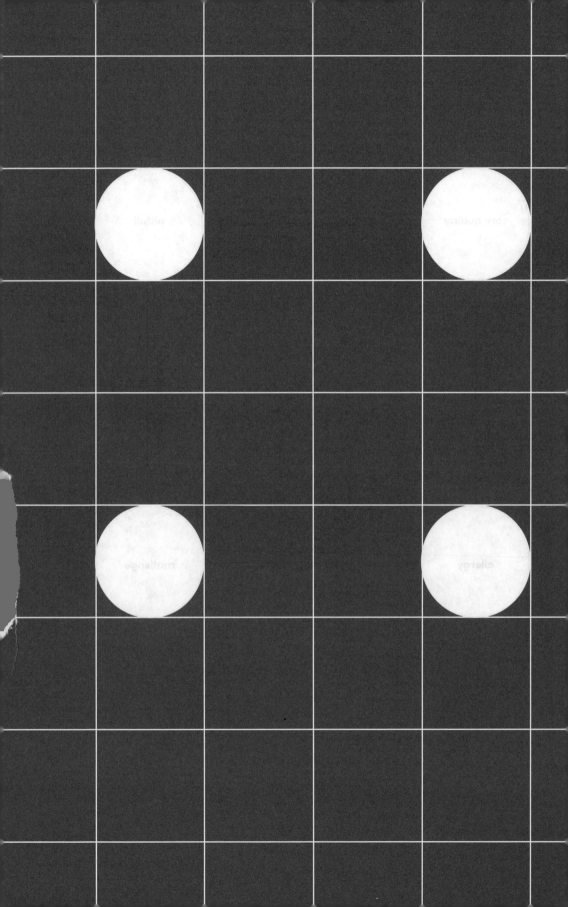

58 Scale walking

ESSENCE Scaling Questions is a technique from the Solution-Focused Therapy as developed by Steve de Shazer and Insoo Kim Berg. It focuses on solutions rather than problems, and uses solution-focused language. The following questions will get you underway. Scale walking steps:

o Describe the problem or challenge and describe why it is a problem.

o Describe what you would prefer to this problem. Make it concrete. Imagine a scale of 1 to 10 and give this scale a name, e.g. the scale of being self-assured. The 10 represents the desired situation and the 1 the place where little has been achieved.

o Describe where you currently are on the scale, e.g. 3. What is already present, that you choose a 3? Itemize five items minimum.

o Are there any past successes, during which things were better?

o Where on the scale would you like to be when you have achieved (e.g. an 8) this goal? What makes it an 8?

o What is the first step you would like to take towards that 8? For example, can you get to a level of 3.5? What is already available in that 3.5? Again, itemize as concretely as possible.

o Hands on and SMART! Make the visualized achievements of step 6 SMART (model 45). For instance, when would you make this step?

o *(optional)* Buy a postcard card or something else that symbolizes this step.

The effect of this model will be that participants will feel empowerment through the interventions of the Solution-Focused Therapy, having a clearer view of their needs. This also contributes to a motivation for action.

EXPERIENCE The scaling questions can be used in caucus, for instance during the exploration phase with a participant feeling powerless. The scaling method focuses on what they *themselves* can do to change the situation. This leads to a feeling of empowerment, causing a shift from 'pinpointing what the other should do', towards what you can do yourself. Another use is during the final phase of mediation, but this is riskier. The question then is what on the way to the desired situation (as defined in the settlement agreement) could be your next, smallest, step towards that situation, starting tomorrow?

EXPLORE Shazer, Steve de and I. Kim Berg. *More Than Miracles: The State of the Art of Solution-Focused Brief Therapy*. New York: Haworth Press 2007.

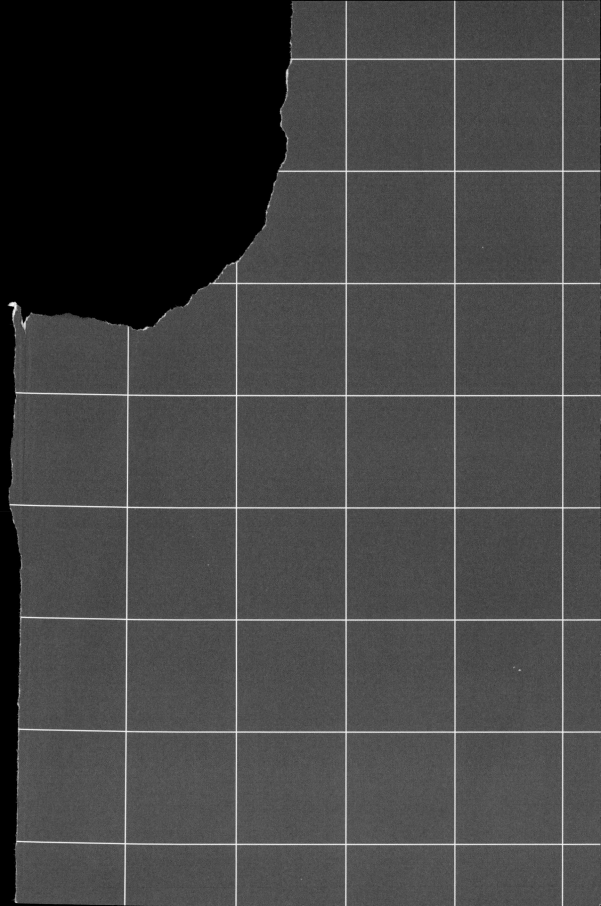

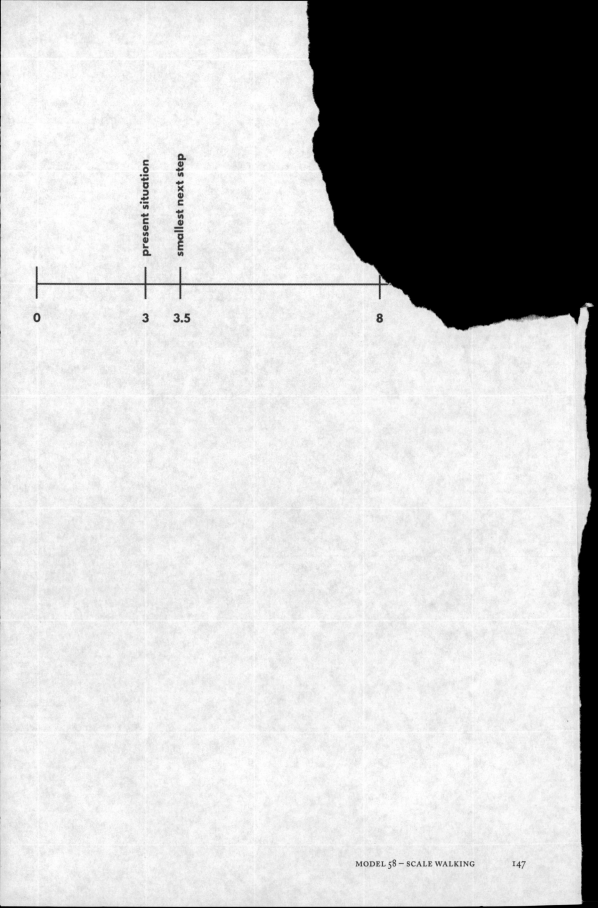

present situation

smallest next step

0   3   3.5   8